Mathematics for the IB Diploma
Higher Level Topic 9
Sets, Relations and Groups

Hugh Neill and Douglas Quadling

Series Editor Hugh Neill

CAMBRIDGE
UNIVERSITY PRESS

CAMBRIDGE UNIVERSITY PRESS
Cambridge, New York, Melbourne, Madrid, Cape Town, Singapore, São Paulo, Delhi

Cambridge University Press
The Edinburgh Building, Cambridge CB2 8RU, UK

www.cambridge.org
Information on this title: www.cambridge.org/9780521714624

First published 2007

A catalogue record for this publication is available from the British Library

ISBN   978-0-521-71462-4 paperback

The authors and the publishers are grateful to the following examination boards for permission to reproduce
questions from past examination papers, identified in the text as follows.
OCR   Oxford, Cambridge and RSA Examinations
IBO   International Baccalaureate Organization
The authors, and not the examination boards, are responsible for the method and accuracy of the answers
to examination questions given; these may not necessarily constitute the only possible solutions.

This material has been developed independently of the International Baccalaureate Organization (IBO).
This text is in no way connected with, nor endorsed by, the IBO.

Contents

Introduction

Sets, Relations and Groups has been written especially for the International Baccalaureate Mathematics HL and FM examinations. This book covers the syllabus for Topic 9.

Chapters 1 to 7 should be studied in sequence, but Chapter 8, on the algebra of sets, can be studied any time after working through Chapter 1. There is a small amount of material which extends a topic beyond the syllabus as printed, with the aim of enhancing students' appreciation of the subject. This is indicated by an asterisk (*) at the appropriate place in the text.

Occasionally within the text paragraphs appear in *this type style*. These paragraphs are usually outside the main stream of the mathematical argument, but may help to give insight, or suggest extra work or different approaches.

There are plenty of exercises throughout. At the end of the book there is a Review exercise which includes some questions from past International Baccalaureate examinations, but on a different syllabus. At the time of writing, there are few current versions of the Higher Level examinations, so there is no backlog of examination questions on the newer parts of the syllabus.

The author thanks the International Baccalaureate Organization (IBO) and Oxford, Cambridge and RSA Examinations (OCR) for permission to reproduce IBO and OCR intellectual property and Cambridge University Press for their help in producing this book. Particular thanks are due to Sharon Dunkley, for her help and advice. However, the responsibility for the text, and for any errors, remains with the author.

1 The language of sets

This chapter is really a reminder about sets. You probably know most of this material already, and you may wish to use the chapter for reference rather than work through it systematically. When you have completed it, you should

- know that a set needs to be defined so that you can tell clearly whether or not a given element belongs to the set
- be able to list the elements of a finite set
- know the meanings of the symbols $\in$, $\notin$, and the bracket notation for sets
- know the meaning of and notation for the empty set
- know the meaning of and notation for intersection, union, set difference and Cartesian product of two sets
- be able to prove that two sets are equal.

1.1 What is a set?

A **set** is a collection of things; the things are called **elements** or **members** of the set. Sets will be denoted by capital letters such as A, B and S.

A set is determined by its elements. To define a set you can either list its elements or you can describe the elements in words, provided you do so unambiguously. When you define a set, there must never be any uncertainty about what its elements are. If there is no uncertainty, the set is said to be **well-defined**.

If you say for example that the set A consists precisely of the numbers 1, 2 and 3 or alternatively, that 1, 2 and 3 are the elements of A, then it is clear that 4 is not an element of A.

The symbol $\in$ is used to designate 'is an element of' or 'belongs to'; the symbol $\notin$ means 'is not an element of' or 'does not belong to'. So $1 \in A$ means that 1 is an element of A, and $4 \notin A$ means that 4 is not a element of A.

There are some sets, in particular sets of numbers, which will be used so frequently that it is helpful to have some special names for them.

Set of numbers	Symbol	Positive only
Integers	$\mathbb{Z}$	$\mathbb{Z}^+$
Natural numbers, including 0	$\mathbb{N}$	
Rational numbers	$\mathbb{Q}$	$\mathbb{Q}^+$
Real numbers	$\mathbb{R}$	$\mathbb{R}^+$
Complex numbers	$\mathbb{C}$	Not applicable

1.2 Describing sets

When you list the elements of a set, it is usual to put them into curly brackets $\{\ \}$, sometimes called **braces**. For example, the set A consisting of the elements 2, 3 and 4 can be written $A = \{2,3,4\}$. The order in which the elements are written doesn't matter. The set $\{2,4,3\}$ is identical to the set $\{2,3,4\}$, and $A = \{2,3,4\} = \{2,4,3\}$.

If you wrote $A = \{2,2,3,4\}$, it would be the same as saying that $A = \{2,3,4\}$. A set is determined by its *distinct* elements, and any repetition in the list of elements should be avoided.

Two sets A and B are called **equal** if and only if they have the same elements.

Using the brace notation, you can write $\mathbb{Z} = \{\ldots,-2,-1,0,1,2,\ldots\}$.

Another way to describe a set involves specifying properties of its elements. For example,

$$A = \{n \mid n \in \mathbb{Z}, 2 \le n \le 4\}$$

means that A is the set of all elements n such that n is an integer and $2 \le n \le 4$. The symbol $\mid$ means 'such that'. To the left of the symbol $\mid$ you are told what a typical element is, while to the right you are given a rule or rules which the typical element must satisfy.

So in A, the elements are the integers which lie between 2 and 4 inclusive. Therefore $A = \{2,3,4\}$.

Sometimes, if there is no room for misunderstanding, you might see in other books the set A of the preceding paragraph defined as

$$A = \{n \in \mathbb{Z}, 2 \le n \le 4\}$$

but that won't be done in this book.

As another example of this notation, the set of rational numbers, $\mathbb{Q}$ (for quotients), can be described as

$$\mathbb{Q} = \left\{ \frac{m}{n} \mid m, n \in \mathbb{Z}, n \ne 0 \right\}.$$

Thus a typical element has the form $\dfrac{m}{n}$, where m and n are integers, and $n \ne 0$.

One more set involving integers will be useful: $\mathbb{Z}_n = \{0,1,2,\ldots,n-1\}$. It may look odd that this set does not contain n, but it does have n members.

Example 1.2.1
List, where possible, the members of each of the following sets.
(a) $A = \{$letters in the word 'sets'$\}$
(b) $B = \{x \mid x \in \mathbb{Q}, x^2 = 4\}$
(c) $C = \{n \mid n \in \mathbb{Z}, n = 4m \text{ where } m \in \mathbb{Z}\}$
(d) $D = \{x \mid x \in \mathbb{R}, x > 1\}$
(e) $E = \{$molecules $\mid$ they were part of the dying breath of Julius Caesar$\}$
     (a)   The letters of the word 'sets' are s, e, t and s. But to say that $A = \{$s, e, t, s$\}$ would be incorrect, because the letter s is repeated.

     Putting the letters in the set into alphabetical order gives $A = \{$e, s, t$\}$.

(b) If $x^2 = 4$ then $x = 2$ or $x = -2$. Both 2 and -2 are rational ($2 = \dfrac{2}{1}$ and $-2 = \dfrac{-2}{1}$), so

$B = \{-2, 2\}$.

(c) C is a set of integers each of which is $4 \times$ (another integer m).

So $C = \{0, \pm 4, \pm 8, \pm 12, \ldots\}$.

(d) This is a well-defined set – you know whether or not a given object is an element of the set – but it is not possible to list it because there is no smallest number in the set.

(e) This is not a well-defined set. There is no method of deciding whether a given molecule was, or was not, part of Julius Caesar's dying breath.

In Example 1.2.1, the numbers of elements in A and B are 3 and 2 respectively. A and B are examples of finite sets, whereas C and D have an infinite number of elements and are examples of infinite sets. The number of elements in a set S is denoted by $n(S)$, so for the sets of Example 1.2.1, $n(A) = 3$, $n(B) = 2$ and $n(\mathbb{Z}_n) = n$; however, in the last case the different use of 'n' is unfortunate, and it will be avoided.

A set with a finite number of elements is called **finite**; sets which are not finite are called **infinite**.

A set with no elements is said to be **empty**. It is usually denoted by $\varnothing$, but it can also be written using the braces notation as $\{\ \}$.

The set which contains all the elements under discussion is called the **universal set** and denoted by U. Every other set will be a subset of U.

Often it is obvious what the universal set is. If you are working with real numbers or complex numbers it is likely to be $\mathbb{R}$ or $\mathbb{C}$ respectively. But if it is not obvious, you will be told the universal set explicitly.

Exercise 1A

1 List the elements of the following sets, stating whether the sets are finite or infinite.
   (a) A is the set of positive factors of 32.
   (b) B is the set of outcomes when an ordinary dice is thrown.
   (c) $C = \{x \mid x \in \mathbb{N}, x^2 = 2\}$
   (d) $D = \{x \mid x \in \mathbb{R}^+, x^2 = 2\}$
   (e) $E = \{x \mid x \in \mathbb{R}, x^2 = 2\}$
   (f) $F = \{n \mid n \in \mathbb{Z}, n = 4p + 5q \text{ for some } p, q \in \mathbb{Z}\}$
   (g) $G = \{n \mid n \in \mathbb{Z}, n = 4p + 6q \text{ for some } p, q \in \mathbb{Z}\}$
   (h) $H = \{r \mid r \in \mathbb{Z}_8, r \geq 4\}$

2 Some of the following sets are not defined properly in the sense that it is not clear whether a given element belongs to the set or not. Identify these sets.

(a) The set of prime numbers.

(b) People in the world whose birthday is on 1 April.

(c) $A = \{x \mid x \in \mathbb{Z}, x$ is the digit in the 1000th place in the decimal expansion of $\pi\}$

3 The notation $2\mathbb{Z}$ is used to mean the set $\{2n \mid n \in \mathbb{Z}\}$. List the set $2\mathbb{Z}$. List also the members of $\mathbb{Z}$ which are not members of $2\mathbb{Z}$.

1.3 Subsets

In Question 2(a) of Exercise 1A, all the elements in the set of prime numbers $\{2, 3, 5, 7, ...\}$ are also members of $\mathbb{N}$. When this happens, the set $\{2, 3, 5, 7, ...\}$ is called a subset of $\mathbb{N}$. More generally, if all the elements of a set A are also elements of another set B, then A is called a **subset** of B. In this case you write $A \subseteq B$.

You can see from the definition of subset that $A \subseteq A$ for every set A.

Notice that the notation $A \subseteq B$ suggests the notation for inequalities, $a \leq b$. This analogy is intentional and helpful. However, you mustn't take the analogy too far: for any two real numbers you have either $a \leq b$ or $b \leq a$, but the same is not true for sets. For example, for the sets $A = \{1\}$ and $B = \{2\}$ neither $A \subseteq B$ nor $B \subseteq A$ is true.

The notation $A \subset B$ is taken to mean that A is a **proper subset** of B, that is $A \subseteq B$ and $A \neq B$. Thus while A is a subset of A, it is not a proper subset of A. A set is not a proper subset of itself.

Summing up:

> Let A and B be sets. Then
>
> - if $x \in A \implies x \in B$, then $A \subseteq B$
>
> - if $x \in A \implies x \in B$ and $A \neq B$, then $A \subset B$.
>
> In the first case, A is a **subset** of B.
>
> In the second case, A is a **proper subset** of B.

Example 1.3.1

$U = \{\text{letters of the alphabet}\}$, $A = \{x \in U \mid x$ is a letter of the word 'table'$\}$,
$B = \{x \in U \mid x$ is a letter of the word 'bleat'$\}$, $C = \{x \in B \mid x$ is a letter of the word 'Beatle'$\}$ and
$D = \{x \in U \mid x$ is a letter of the word 'beetle'$\}$.

Which of the sets, U, A, B, C and D are
(a) equal to each other,   (b) subsets of each other,   (c) proper subsets of each other?

Listing the sets gives $A = \{a,b,e,l,t\}$, $B = \{a,b,e,l,t\}$, $C = \{a,b,e,l,t\}$ and $D = \{b,e,l,t\}$. You can then answer the questions by examining these sets.

(a) $A = B = C$.

(b) $U \subseteq U$, $A \subseteq U$, $B \subseteq U$, $C \subseteq U$, $D \subseteq U$, $A \subseteq A$, $B \subseteq A$, $C \subseteq A$, $D \subseteq A$, $A \subseteq B$, $B \subseteq B$, $C \subseteq B$, $D \subseteq B$, $A \subseteq C$, $B \subseteq C$, $C \subseteq C$, $D \subseteq C$ and $D \subseteq D$.

(c) $A \subset U$, $B \subset U$, $C \subset U$, $D \subset U$, $D \subset A$, $D \subset B$ and $D \subset C$.

1.4   Venn diagrams

Fig. 1.1 and Fig. 1.2 show ways of illustrating sets. They are called **Venn diagrams** after the Englishman John Venn (1834–1923).

The set A is drawn as a circle (or an oval), and x, which is an element of A, is drawn as a point inside A. The outside rectangle indicates the universal set. Fig. 1.1 represents $x \in A$.

In Fig. 1.2, every point inside A is also inside B; this represents the statement that A is a subset of B, or $A \subset B$.

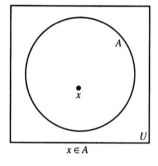

$x \in A$

Fig. 1.1

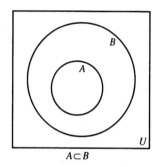

$A \subset B$

Fig. 1.2

These diagrams can be helpful for understanding, seeing and suggesting relationships, but be warned; they can also sometimes be misleading. For example, in Fig. 1.2, the question of whether or not $A = B$ is left open. The fact that in the diagram there are points outside A and inside B does not mean that there are necessarily elements in B which are not in A. Take care when using Venn diagrams!

1.5   Operations on sets: complementation, intersection, union and set difference

In Exercise 1A Question 3 you were asked to list the members of the set $\mathbb{Z}$ which are not members of $2\mathbb{Z}$. As $\mathbb{Z} = \{0, \pm 1, \pm 2, ...\}$ and $2\mathbb{Z} = \{0, \pm 2, \pm 4, ...\}$ the required set was $\{\pm 1, \pm 3, \pm 5, ...\}$. But so far, there is no name for it.

Let A be a set. Then the set of elements in the universal set U which are not in A is called the **complement** of A and denoted by A', pronounced 'A prime, or A dash'.

In Fig. 1.3 the shaded region outside A but within the universal set U illustrates A'.

Formally this is written as:

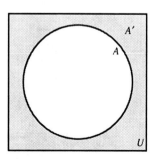

Fig. 1.3

> Let A be a set, and let U be the universal set.
>
> Then $A' = \{x \in U \mid x \notin A\}$ is called the **complement** of A.

Example 1.5.1

List the members of A' in the following cases.

(a) $U = \{\text{letters of the alphabet}\}$, $A = \{\text{consonants}\}$

(b) $A = \{n \mid n \in \mathbb{N}, n = 2m + 1 \text{ where } m \in \mathbb{N}\}$

    (a)   Assuming that y is a consonant, $A' = \{a, e, i, o, u\}$.

    (b)   The elements of A are those which are of the form $2m + 1$ where $m \in \mathbb{N}$. So $A = \{1, 3, 5, ...\}$. In this case, the universal set is not given explicitly, but you should assume that it is $\mathbb{N}$, as that is the set used in the definition of A.

            So $A' = \{0, 2, 4, ...\}$.

Now consider $A = \{x \mid x \in \mathbb{N}, x \text{ is a factor of } 12\}$ and $B = \{x \mid x \in \mathbb{N}, x \text{ is a factor of } 15\}$.

Thus $A = \{1, 2, 3, 4, 6, 12\}$ and $B = \{1, 3, 5, 15\}$.

As you can see, there are elements, 1 and 3, which are members of both sets. These elements, 1 and 3, themselves form a set, called the **intersection** of A and B.

> Let A and B be sets.
>
> Then the set $\{x \mid x \in A \text{ and } x \in B\}$ is called the **intersection** of A and B and denoted by $A \cap B$.
>
> It is clear from the definition that $A \cap B = B \cap A$.

$A \cap B$ is pronounced 'A intersection B'.

Going back to $A = \{1, 2, 3, 4, 6, 12\}$ and $B = \{1, 3, 5, 15\}$, you can also construct a new set of elements which are in either A or B (or both).

This would be the set $\{1, 2, 3, 4, 5, 6, 12, 15\}$, which is called the **union** of the sets A and B.

> Let A and B be sets.
>
> Then the set $\{x \mid x \in A \text{ or } x \in B\}$ is called the **union** of A and B and denoted by $A \cup B$.
>
> It is clear from the definition that $A \cup B = B \cup A$.

Note that in the expression $x \in A$ or $x \in B$, the word 'or' is inclusive, and that $x \in A$ or $x \in B$ means $x \in A$ or $x \in B$ or both.

Figs. 1.4 and 1.5 are Venn diagrams which illustrate the intersection and union of the sets A and B.

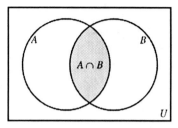

The shaded region is $A \cap B$.

Fig. 1.4

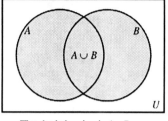

The shaded region is $A \cup B$.

Fig. 1.5

Fig. 1.6 shows a Venn diagram for illustrating three sets. However, don't even think of drawing a Venn diagram for four sets or more as the picture gets much too cluttered.

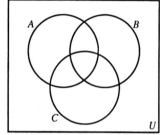

Fig. 1.6

Example 1.5.2

Draw Venn diagrams to illustrate the sets $A \cup B'$, $A' \cap B$ and $A' \cap B \cap C$.

The solutions are shown in Figs. 1.7, 1.8 and 1.9.

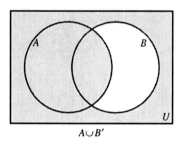

$A \cup B'$

Fig. 1.7

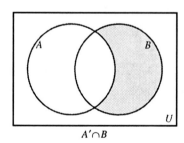

$A' \cap B$

Fig. 1.8

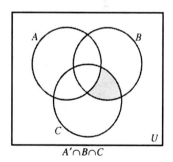

$A' \cap B \cap C$

Fig. 1.9

Example 1.5.3

Let $A = \{2,3,4\}$, $B = \{4,5,6\}$ and $C = \{6,7,8\}$. List the sets $A \cap B$, $A \cup C$ and $A \cap C$.

$A \cap B$ consists of the elements which are in both A and B, so $A \cap B = \{4\}$.

$A \cup C$ consists of the elements in either A or C, so $A \cup C = \{2,3,4,6,7,8\}$.

$A \cap C = \{\ \} = \varnothing$.

In the third case, when there are no elements common to both of the sets, the sets are said to be **disjoint**.

> Let A and B be sets.
>
> Then if $A \cap B = \varnothing$, the sets A and B are said to be **disjoint**.

The question of whether $\varnothing$ is a subset of A or B is somewhat tricky. If you try to use the definition, you have to decide whether 'if $x \in \varnothing$ then $x \in A$' is true. As there is no element x which belongs to $\varnothing$ it is certainly not possible to find an x to show that the statement 'if $x \in \varnothing$ then $x \in A$' is false. So, conventionally, $\varnothing$ is defined to be a subset of every set A.

> Let A be a set. Then $\varnothing \subseteq A$. If $A \neq \varnothing$, then $\varnothing \subset A$.

Example 1.5.4
(a) Let D be the set of plane rhombuses, and R be the set of plane rectangles. Identify $D \cap R$ and $D \cap R'$.
(b) Let Q be the set of plane quadrilaterals and T be the set of triangles. Identify $Q \cap T$.

(a) $D \cap R$ is the set of those rhombuses which are also rectangles. So $D \cap R$ is the set of squares. $D \cap R'$ are the non-rectangular rhombuses, that is, the rhombuses which are not squares.

Note that if you had been asked to describe $D' \cap R'$ it would have been impossible without knowing the universal set.

(b)   There are no quadrilaterals which are also triangles, so Q and T are disjoint and $Q \cap T = \varnothing$.

Sometimes you need to be able to consider a set without certain members. For example $\mathbb{N} = \{0,1,2,3,...\}$, but if you want to consider the set $\{1,2,3,...\}$, that is $\mathbb{N}$, without the element 0, then $\{1,2,3,...\}$ is called the **set difference** of $\mathbb{N}$ and $\{0\}$.

> Let A and B be sets.
>
> Then the set $\{x \mid x \in A$ and $x \notin B\}$ is called the **set difference** of A and B and denoted by $A \setminus B$.

It is clear from the definition that $A \setminus B = A \cap B'$.

Example 1.5.5
Let $A = \{1,2,3,4,6,12\}$ and $B = \{1,3,5,15\}$. List the sets $A \setminus B$ and $B \setminus A$.

$A \setminus B = \{2,4,6,12\}$ and $B \setminus A = \{5,15\}$.

Exercise 1B

1   Let $A = \{2,4,6,8\}$, $B = \{1,2,4,8\}$, $C = \{1,2,5\}$ and let the universal set be $\mathbb{Z}_9$. List the members of the following sets.

(a) $A \cup B$ (b) $A \cap C$ (c) C' (d) $B \setminus C$

(e) $A \cap C'$ (f) $A' \cup C'$ (g) $B' \cap C'$ (h) $(A \cup B) \setminus C$

2   Let the universal set be the set of triangles, and define the following subsets:
$S = \{\text{scalene triangles}\}$, $I = \{\text{isosceles triangles}\}$, $E = \{\text{equilateral triangles}\}$ and
$R = \{\text{right-angled triangles}\}$. Describe in words or symbols each of the following sets.

(a) $I \cap E$ (b) S' (c) $E \cap R$ (d) $I \setminus E$

(e) $S' \cap E$ (f) $E' \cap R$ (g) $S \cup I$ (h) $R \setminus I$

3   Let the universal set be the set of plane quadrilaterals, and define the subsets $P = \{\text{parallelograms}\}$, $R = \{\text{rectangles}\}$, $D = \{\text{rhombuses}\}$, $S = \{\text{squares}\}$, $K = \{\text{kites}\}$ and $T = \{\text{trapezia}\}$. Describe in words or symbols each of the following sets.

(a) $K \cap D$ (b) $D \cap R$ (c) $K \cap T$ (d) $R \cap P$

1.6 Proving that two sets are equal

To prove that two sets A and B are equal, you have, at this stage, to prove separately that $A \subseteq B$ and that $B \subseteq A$, that is, that every element of A is also an element of B, and vice versa.

Here are some examples of proofs of this type.

Example 1.6.1
Prove that if A and B are sets, then $A \cap B = B \cap A$.

Proof
The proof that $A \cap B = B \cap A$ has two parts: first, to prove that $A \cap B \subseteq B \cap A$; and secondly, to prove that $B \cap A \subseteq A \cap B$.

Proof of $A \cap B \subseteq B \cap A$
Suppose that $x \in A \cap B$. Then

$$x \in A \cap B \;\Rightarrow\; x \in A \text{ and } x \in B$$
$$\Rightarrow\; x \in B \text{ and } x \in A$$
$$\Rightarrow\; x \in B \cap A.$$

Thus $A \cap B \subseteq B \cap A$.

Proof of $B \cap A \subseteq A \cap B$
Suppose that $x \in B \cap A$. Then

$$x \in B \cap A \;\Rightarrow\; x \in B \text{ and } x \in A$$
$$\Rightarrow\; x \in A \text{ and } x \in B$$
$$\Rightarrow\; x \in A \cap B.$$

Thus $B \cap A \subseteq A \cap B$.

As $A \cap B \subseteq B \cap A$ and $B \cap A \subseteq A \cap B$, it follows that $A \cap B = B \cap A$.

$A \cap B = B \cap A$ is called the **commutative** rule for intersection of sets. There is a similar commutative rule for union of sets which you are asked to prove as Question 5 of Exercise 1C.

Example 1.6.2

Prove that if A, B and C are sets, then $(A \cup B) \cup C = A \cup (B \cup C)$.

Proof

The first part is to prove that $(A \cup B) \cup C \subseteq A \cup (B \cup C)$.

Proof of $(A \cup B) \cup C \subseteq A \cup (B \cup C)$

Suppose that $x \in (A \cup B) \cup C$. Then

$$
\begin{aligned}
x \in (A \cup B) \cup C \;&\Rightarrow\; x \in A \cup B \text{ or } x \in C \\
&\Rightarrow\; (x \in A \text{ or } x \in B) \text{ or } x \in C \\
&\Rightarrow\; x \in A \text{ or } x \in B \text{ or } x \in C \\
&\Rightarrow\; x \in A \text{ or } (x \in B \text{ or } x \in C) \\
&\Rightarrow\; x \in A \text{ or } x \in B \cup C \\
&\Rightarrow\; x \in A \cup (B \cup C).
\end{aligned}
$$

Thus $(A \cup B) \cup C \subseteq A \cup (B \cup C)$.

The proof of the second part is similar; it is left for you to prove that

$$A \cup (B \cup C) \subseteq (A \cup B) \cup C.$$

As $(A \cup B) \cup C \subseteq A \cup (B \cup C)$ and $A \cup (B \cup C) \subseteq (A \cup B) \cup C$, it follows that

$$(A \cup B) \cup C = A \cup (B \cup C).$$

This is called the **associative** rule for union of sets. There is a similar associative rule for intersection of sets which you are asked to prove as Question 6 of Exercise 1C.

Example 1.6.3

Prove that, for any sets A and B,

(a) $A \cap A = A$,   (b) $A \cup (A \cap B) = A$.

(a)   **Proof of $A \cap A \subseteq A$**

Suppose that $x \in A \cap A$. Then

$$
\begin{aligned}
x \in A \cap A \;&\Rightarrow\; x \in A \text{ and } x \in A \\
&\Rightarrow\; x \in A.
\end{aligned}
$$

Proof of $A \subseteq A \cap A$

Suppose that $x \in A$.

$$
\begin{aligned}
x \in A \;&\Rightarrow\; x \in A \text{ and } x \in A \\
&\Rightarrow\; x \in A \cap A.
\end{aligned}
$$

As $A \cap A \subseteq A$ and $A \subseteq A \cap A$, it follows that $A \cap A = A$.

(b)   **Proof of $A \cup (A \cap B) \subseteq A$**
Suppose that $x \in A \cup (A \cap B)$. Then

$$x \in A \cup (A \cap B) \;\Rightarrow\; x \in A \text{ or } x \in (A \cap B)$$
$$\Rightarrow\; x \in A \text{ or } (x \in A \text{ and } x \in B).$$

Either way, $x \in A$, so $A \cup (A \cap B) \subseteq A$.

Proof of $A \subseteq A \cup (A \cap B)$
Suppose that $x \in A$. Then

$$x \in A \;\Rightarrow\; x \in A \text{ or } (x \in A \text{ and } x \in B)$$
$$\Rightarrow\; x \in A \text{ or } x \in (A \cap B)$$
$$\Rightarrow\; x \in A \cup (A \cap B).$$

Therefore $A \subseteq A \cup (A \cap B)$.

As $A \cup (A \cap B) \subseteq A$ and $A \subseteq A \cup (A \cap B)$, it follows that $A \cup (A \cap B) = A$.

Example 1.6.3(a) shows that $A \cap A = A$, an example of one of the **tautology** rules.

There is another **tautology** rule in Exercise 1C Question 7.

Example 1.6.3(b) shows that $A \cup (A \cap B) = A$, an example of one of the **absorption** rules.

There is another **absorption** rule in Exercise 1C Question 8.

The tautology and absorption rules will be followed up in Section 8.4.

Here is an example suggested by the Venn diagram in Fig. 1.10.

Example 1.6.4
Prove that, for any sets A and B, if $A \subseteq B$ then $A \cap B = A$.

Proof
In this case the hypothesis that $A \subseteq B$ tells you that if $x \in A$ then $x \in B$. This will be used in appropriate places in the proof that $A \cap B = A$.

Proof of $A \cap B \subseteq A$
Suppose that $x \in A \cap B$. Then

$$x \in A \cap B \;\Rightarrow\; x \in A \text{ and } x \in B$$
$$\Rightarrow\; x \in A.$$

Therefore $A \cap B \subseteq A$.

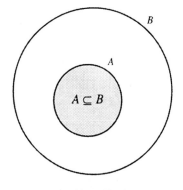

Fig. 1.10

Proof of $A \subseteq A \cap B$

Suppose that $x \in A$. Then

$$x \in A \quad \Rightarrow \quad x \in A \text{ and } x \in B \qquad \text{(since } A \subseteq B \text{ is given)}$$
$$\Rightarrow \quad x \in A \cap B.$$

Hence $A \subseteq A \cap B$.

As $A \cap B \subseteq A$ and $A \subseteq A \cap B$, it follows that $A \cap B = A$.

It is also true that if $A \cap B = A$, then $A \subseteq B$. This is proved as Example 1.6.5.

Example 1.6.5
Prove that if $A \cap B = A$, then $A \subseteq B$.

Proof

Suppose that $x \in A$. Then

$$x \in A \quad \Rightarrow \quad x \in A \text{ and } x \in B \qquad \text{(as } A = A \cap B \text{ is given)}$$
$$\Rightarrow \quad x \in B.$$

Thus $A \subseteq B$.

Notice that Examples 1.6.4 and 1.6.5 together show that the two statements $A \subseteq B$ and $A \cap B = A$ are equivalent because each can be deduced from the other.

It follows that

$$A \subseteq B \quad \Leftrightarrow \quad A \cap B = A.$$

Exercise 1C

1 Draw Venn diagrams to illustrate sets P, Q and $P \cap Q'$. What can you say about P, Q if you know that $P \cap Q' = \varnothing$?

2 Draw Venn diagrams to illustrate sets P, Q and $P \cup Q'$. What can you say about P, Q if you know that $P \cup Q' = Q'$?

3 Write down simpler expressions for each of the following.

(a) $A \cap \varnothing$ (b) $A \cup \varnothing$ (c) $A \cap U$

(d) $A \cup U$ (e) $\varnothing'$ (f) U'

4 Use a Venn diagram to simplify $A \cap (A \cup B')$.

5 Prove algebraically that $A \cup B = B \cup A$.

6 Prove algebraically that $(A \cap B) \cap C = A \cap (B \cap C)$.

7 Prove that for any set A, $A \cup A = A$. This is the other **tautology** rule.

8   Prove that, for any sets A and B, $A \cap (A \cup B) = A$. This is the other **absorption** rule.

9   Prove that if $A \cup B = A$ then $A \cap B' = \varnothing$, and if $A \cap B' = \varnothing$ then $A \cup B = A$.

10 Use a Venn diagram to simplify $(A \cap B \cap C) \cup A' \cup B' \cup C'$.

1.7 The Cartesian product

You are familiar with the idea of coordinates in the plane consisting of ordered pairs of numbers. You are used to plotting points such as $(3,2)$ and $(\sqrt{2}, -\sqrt{2})$ on coordinate axes on graph paper. Each of the numbers in such a coordinate pair comes from a set: when you plot graphs this set is usually the real numbers $\mathbb{R}$. The set of all pairs of coordinates such as $(3,2)$ and $(\sqrt{2}, -\sqrt{2})$ is called $\mathbb{R} \times \mathbb{R}$, meaning that the first number comes from the set $\mathbb{R}$, as does the second number. The notation $\mathbb{R}^2$ is often used for $\mathbb{R} \times \mathbb{R}$, especially in the context of vectors. The Cartesian product generalises this idea.

> Let A and B be sets.
>
> Then the set $\{(a,b) \mid a \in A, b \in B\}$ is called the **Cartesian product** of A and B and denoted by $A \times B$.

The Cartesian product is named after the Frenchman René Descartes (1596–1650).

Example 1.7.1
Suppose that $A = \{2,3,4\}$ and $B = \{x, y\}$. List the elements of $A \times B$.

$$A \times B = \{(2,x),(2,y),(3,x),(3,y),(4,x),(4,y)\}.$$

Notice that the set $B \times A$ is not the same as $A \times B$, because

$$B \times A = \{(x,2),(y,2),(x,3),(y,3),(x,4),(y,4)\},$$

so the order of the sets in a Cartesian product matters.

Notice also that neither A nor B is a subset of $A \times B$. The set $A \times B$ consists of pairs: the elements of A and B are not pairs, so do not belong to $A \times B$.

If you roll an ordinary fair dice, then the set D of possible outcomes can be written as a set

$$D = \{1,2,3,4,5,6\}.$$

If you roll a pair of dice, and you can distinguish between the dice, then the outcomes can be written as the Cartesian product $D \times D$, with 36 elements, where

$$D \times D = \{(1,1),(1,2),\ldots,(1,6),(2,1),\ldots,(6,5),(6,6)\}.$$

This idea is commonly used in statistics, where the set $D \times D$ is called a sample space.

Example 1.7.2
Suppose that A has m elements and B has n elements. How many elements does $A \times B$ have?

Let $A = \{a_1, a_2, a_3, \dots, a_m\}$ and $B = \{b_1, b_2, b_3, \dots, b_n\}$.

Then the elements of $A \times B$ are

$$\left\{ \begin{array}{cccc} (a_1, b_1) & (a_1, b_2) & \cdots & (a_1, b_n) \\ (a_2, b_1) & (a_2, b_2) & \cdots & (a_2, b_n) \\ & & & \\ (a_m, b_1) & (a_m, b_2) & \cdots & (a_m, b_n) \end{array} \right\}.$$

When you count the elements, you see that there are mn of them.

You can also extend the definition of the Cartesian product in an obvious way to produce a Cartesian product of more than two sets.

Exercise 1D

1   Let C be the set of outcomes when a coin is tossed, and let D be the outcomes when a dice is rolled.
    (a) List $C \times D$.   (b) List $D \times C$.

2   Mark each of the following statements about the sets A and B true or false.
    (a) The set $A \times B$ always has a finite number of elements.
    (b) You cannot form the direct product $A \times B$ if just one of A and B is infinite.

3   Write a definition for the set $A \times B \times C$. If $\mathbb{Z}_2 = \{0,1\}$, use your definition to write out the elements of $\mathbb{Z}_2 \times \mathbb{Z}_2 \times \mathbb{Z}_2$.

4   Prove that $\mathbb{Z} \times \mathbb{Z} \subseteq \mathbb{Q} \times \mathbb{Q}$.

5   You can interpret the set $\mathbb{R} \times \mathbb{R}$ as all the points on an infinite sheet of paper. How would you interpret $\mathbb{Z} \times \mathbb{Z}$?

2 Equivalence relations

This chapter introduces the idea of a relation between members of a set. When you have completed it, you should

- know and be able to use the definition of an equivalence relation on a set
- know the meaning of 'reflexive', 'symmetric' and 'transitive' in the context of relations
- know the definition of a partition
- know that an equivalence relation on a set partitions the set into equivalence classes and be able to identify them.

2.1 Relations

This section just consists of an example followed by a short exercise to set the scene for later in the chapter. Keep the results for reference.

Example 2.1.1
On paper draw axes from 1 to 6 in each direction, as in Fig. 2.1. The axes are labelled a and b.

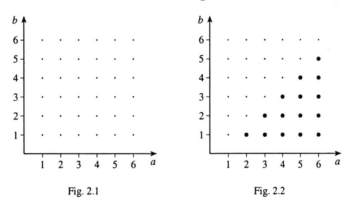

Fig. 2.1   Fig. 2.2

This is the set $D \times D$, where $D = \{1,2,3,4,5,6\}$. (Think of D as standing for dice.)

Take a point (a,b) in $D \times D$. If $a > b$, then a and b will be said to be 'related', and written aRb. In Fig. 2.2, each point (a,b) which has $a > b$ is marked with a blob. Thus the points aRb in $D \times D$ are marked.

What are the values of a which are related to each b? That is, for $b = 1$, what is the set $\{a \mid a \in D, aR1\}$? Call this set $\overline{1}$.

Then $\overline{1}$ is the set of values of a in Fig. 2.2 with a blob to the right of 1 on the b-axis. There are five of them, so $\overline{1} = \{2,3,4,5,6\}$.

$\overline{2}$ is the set of values of a with a blob to the right of 2. There are four such values, so $\overline{2} = \{3,4,5,6\}$.

Similarly, $\overline{3} = \{4,5,6\}$, $\overline{4} = \{5,6\}$, $\overline{5} = \{6\}$, $\overline{6} = \{\ \}$.

Exercise 2A

1 Make a copy of $D \times D$, and repeat Example 2.1.1, including finding $\overline{1}, \overline{2}, \dots, \overline{6}$ when

    (a) aRb stands for $a + b$ is an even number,

    (b) aRb stands for $2a - b$ is divisible by 3,

    (c) aRb stands for $a - b$ is divisible by 3,

    (d) aRb stands for ab leaves a remainder of 1 when divided by 7.

2.2 Looking at results

Example 2.1.1 and the four parts of Exercise 2A Question 1 have very different patterns of blobs and lists of sets from one another. In particular in part (a) when $a + b$ is an even number and in part (c) when $a - b$ is divisible by 3 you get symmetrical patterns of blobs in $D \times D$.. You also get symmetrical patterns in parts (b) and (d) but with an important difference: in these cases at least one member of $D \times D$ is not related to itself.

The lists $\overline{1}, \overline{2}, \dots, \overline{6}$ are also very different. In part (a) $\overline{1} = \overline{3} = \overline{5} = \{1,3,5\}$ and $\overline{2} = \overline{4} = \overline{6} = \{2,4,6\}$, and in part (c), $\overline{1} = \overline{4} = \{1,4\}$, $\overline{2} = \overline{5} = \{2,5\}$ and $\overline{3} = \overline{6} = \{3,6\}$. This separation into distinct subsets occurs also in part (b), with the important difference that $1 \notin \overline{1}$, $2 \notin \overline{2}$, $4 \notin \overline{4}$ and $5 \notin \overline{5}$. Similarly, in part (d), $2 \notin \overline{2}$, $3 \notin \overline{3}$, $4 \notin \overline{4}$ and $5 \notin \overline{5}$.

In the remainder of this chapter, the focus will be on the cases like parts (a) and (c), but in rather more general terms.

2.3 Some definitions

In Section 2.1, the word 'related' was not clearly defined. If A is a set, then a **relation** R on A is defined to be a subset of $A \times A$.

This definition turns out to be not especially helpful, except for saying clearly what a relation is: the notation aRb is better, and is connected to the subset idea above by saying that

$$(a,b) \in R \quad \Leftrightarrow \quad aRb.$$

In the remainder of the book, the aRb notation is used for a relation.

In the next section, the idea of an equivalence relation is explored informally.

2.4 Equivalence relations

An equivalence relation is a mathematical way of modelling 'sameness'.

Consider, for example, the set of lower and upper case letters of the alphabet, $\{a,b,c,\dots,A,B,C,\dots\}$. You may wish, for some purposes, to think of e and E as the 'same' as each other; for other purposes, you may wish to think of the lower case letters as the 'same' as each other and for yet other purposes, you may wish to think of vowels as the 'same' as each other. When two things are the 'same' in some way, in that they share some particular property, they are called 'equivalent' with regard to that property. The notion of an equivalence relation provides a means of discussing this abstractly, without referring to any particular property.

In geometry, it is often convenient to think of triangles which are congruent to one another as equivalent, even though they may be located in different places and therefore, strictly, different triangles.

In a school, it is sometimes useful to think of the students in each class as equivalent. Then you have divided the students of the school into subsets matched with the classes.

In Exercise 2A Question 1(a), the values of a divided themselves into subsets which are the even and odd numbers, and in Question 1(c) they were those numbers which leave remainders 1, 2 and 0 on division by 3. If you had found the values of b which were related to given values of a you would have found the same results.

> An **equivalence relation** on a set A is a relation R with all three of the following properties.
>
> - xRx for all $x \in A$ Reflexive property
>
> - if xRy, then yRx Symmetric property
>
> - if xRy and yRz, then xRz Transitive property

Here are some examples of relations on a set; some are equivalence relations and some are not.

Example 2.4.1

Let $A = \{$people living in the UK$\}$ and let xRy if $x, y \in A$ and if x and y were born in the same calendar year. Show that R is an equivalence relation. What is the subset of those people related to you?

Clearly x was born in the same year as x, so xRx and R is reflexive.

If x was born in the same year as y, then y was born in the same year as x. So R is symmetric.

And if x was born in the same year as y, and y was born in the same year as z, then x was born in the same year as z. So R is transitive.

Therefore R is an equivalence relation on A.

If you are called a, then $\bar{a}$ is the subset of people related to you, that is the set of people living in the UK who were born in the same year as you.

In fact, A is divided into subsets corresponding to calendar years, each calendar year containing the people who were born in that year.

Example 2.4.2

Show that the relation R on $\mathbb{Z}$ defined by xRy if $x - y$ is divisible by 3 is an equivalence relation. List the sets $\bar{0}$, $\bar{1}$ and $\bar{2}$.

Since $x - x = 0$ which is divisible by 3, xRx. So R is reflexive.

If xRy, then $x - y$ is divisible by 3. Therefore $y - x = -(x - y)$ is divisible by 3, so yRx. So R is symmetric.

Finally if xRy and yRz, then both $x - y$ and $y - z$ are divisible by 3. Therefore $x - y = 3m$ and $y - z = 3n$ for some integers m and n. Adding these two equations gives $x - z = 3(m + n)$, so $x - z$ is divisible by 3. So xRz and R is transitive.

Hence R is an equivalence relation.

In this case, $\bar{0} = \{0, \pm 3, \pm 6, \ldots\}$, $\bar{1} = \{\ldots, -5, -2, 1, 4, 7, \ldots\}$ and $\bar{2} = \{\ldots, -4, -1, 2, 5, 8, \ldots\}$.

Example 2.4.3

Show that the relation on $A = \{\text{people living in the UK}\}$, given by xRy if x is a friend of y, is not an equivalence relation.

In this case, R is not an equivalence relation because you cannot guarantee that the transitive relation holds. x can be friendly with y, and y can be friendly with z without x being friendly with z. So the transitive law doesn't hold and 'is a friend of' is not an equivalence relation.

Example 2.4.4

Define the relation R on $\mathbb{Z}$, by xRy if 5 divides $2x - y$. Show that R is not an equivalence relation on $\mathbb{Z}$.

R is not an equivalence relation because x is not related to x for all $x \in \mathbb{Z}$. If $x = 1$, then $2x - x = x = 1$, and 5 does not divide 1. Hence $1R1$ is false.

In fact, this relation is not symmetric or transitive, as well as not being reflexive, but you only need to show that one of the conditions fails to show R is not an equivalence relation.

In Examples 2.4.1 and 2.4.2, in which the relations were equivalence relations, the underlying sets, A and $\mathbb{Z}$, were divided into subsets containing elements which were related to each other. This idea leads to the following definition and theorem.

The set $\bar{a} = \{x \in A : xRa\}$ is called the **equivalence class** of a.

Theorem 2.1   Let R be an equivalence relation on a set A. Then
(a)   for each $a \in A$, $a \in \bar{a}$
(b)   for each $a, b \in A$, aRb if, and only if, $\bar{a} = \bar{b}$.

This theorem says first, that a is in its own equivalence class, and secondly, if a is related to b, then the equivalence classes of a and b are identical, and vice versa.

Proof

(a)   Since R is an equivalence relation, aRa, so $a \in \bar{a}$.

(b)   **Proof of 'if'**

Suppose that $\bar{a} = \bar{b}$. Then $\bar{a} \subseteq \bar{b}$. From part (a), $a \in \bar{a}$, so $\bar{a} \subseteq \bar{b}$. Therefore aRb .

Proof of 'only if'

Let aRb . First suppose that $x \in \bar{a}$, so that xRa. Then xRa and aRb, so, by the transitive rule xRb. Therefore $x \in \bar{b}$. So if $x \in \bar{a}$, $x \in \bar{b}$. So $\bar{a} \subseteq \bar{b}$.

Now suppose that $x \in \bar{b}$, so xRb. But, aRb, and, by the symmetric rule, bRa. Hence xRb and bRa, so, by the transitive rule, xRa, giving $x \in \bar{a}$. So if $x \in \bar{b}$, $x \in \bar{a}$, so $\bar{b} \subseteq \bar{a}$.

Therefore, as $\bar{a} \subseteq \bar{b}$ and $\bar{b} \subseteq \bar{a}$, $\bar{a} = \bar{b}$.

In Examples 2.4.1 and 2.4.2, and in Exercise 2A parts (a) and (c) the subsets into which A and $\mathbb{Z}$ were divided were disjoint: they had no elements in common. This is the essence of the idea of a partition.

2.5   Partitions

A **partition** of a set A is a division of A into subsets such that every element of A is in exactly one of the subsets.

The 'exactly' part of the definition ensures that the subsets in a partition are disjoint.

Theorem 2.2   For any equivalence relation R on a set A, the set of equivalence classes forms a partition of A.

Proof

Every element of A is in at least one equivalence class by part (a) of Theorem 2.1. This ensures that no element is 'left out in the cold'.

It remains to prove that each element is in exactly one equivalence class. To do this, the strategy is to suppose that there is an element x which is in two distinct equivalence classes, and then to show that if this is the case, the equivalence classes are identical, and are therefore not distinct. This establishes a contradiction.

Let $a, b \in A$ and suppose that the equivalence classes of a and b are not disjoint, that is, $\bar{a} \cap \bar{b}$ is non-empty. The aim is now to prove that $\bar{a} = \bar{b}$.

As $\bar{a} \cap \bar{b}$ is non-empty, there exists an element $x \in A$, such that $x \in \bar{a}$ and $x \in \bar{b}$.

Therefore xRa and xRb. Therefore, as R is symmetric, aRx.

As aRx and xRb, by the transitive rule, aRb. Therefore, by part (b) of Theorem 2.1, $\bar{a} = \bar{b}$.

Therefore either $\bar{a}$ and $\bar{b}$ are identical or they are disjoint.

Hence the set of equivalence classes is a partition.

This is an important result.

Let R be an equivalence relation on a set A.

The set $\bar{a} = \{x \in A : xRa\}$ is called the **equivalence class** of a.

The equivalence classes **partition** A.

Example 2.5.1
In Example 2.4.1, $A = \{\text{people living in the UK}\}$ and it was shown that the relation R defined so that xRy if x and y were born in the same calendar year is an equivalence relation. Find the equivalence classes corresponding to R.

The equivalence classes are those people living in the UK who were born in the same calendar year.

Example 2.5.2
In Example 2.4.2, where the relation R on $\mathbb{Z}$ defined by xRy if $x - y$ is divisible by 3 was shown to be an equivalence relation, find the equivalence classes.

The equivalence classes consist of members of $\mathbb{Z}$ which leave the same remainder on division by 3.

Example 2.5.3
Let $A =$ the set of towns in Great Britain. Let a and b be towns, and let aRb if a and b are in the same county. Identify the equivalence classes.

Each town a is in the same county as itself, so aRa and R is reflexive.

Let a and b be two towns in Great Britain. Then, if aRb, a and b are in the same county. But then b and a are in the same county, so bRa and R is symmetric.

Finally, let a, b and c be three towns in Great Britain. If aRb then a and b are in the same county, and if bRc then b and c are in the same county. It follows that a and c are in the same county, so aRc and R is transitive

The equivalence classes are the counties. Fig. 2.3 shows Great Britain partitioned into counties.

Great Britain partitioned into equivalence classes

Fig. 2.3

Exercise 2B

1 Show that each of the following relations is an equivalence relation. In each case identify the equivalence classes.

(a) On $\mathbb{R}^2 \setminus \{(0,0)\}$, $(a,b) R(c,d)$ if $ad - bc = 0$

(b) On $\mathbb{Q}$, $(p/q) R(r/s)$ if $ps - qr = 0$

(c) On $\mathbb{Z}$, xRy if $x - y$ is divisible by 2

(d) On $\mathbb{Z}$, xRy if $2x + y$ is divisible by 3

(e) On $\mathbb{Z}$, xRy if $|x| = |y|$

2 Decide whether each of the following relations is an equivalence relation, giving the equivalence classes where appropriate.

(a) On $\mathbb{Z}$, xRy if $x - y$ is the square of an integer

(b) On $\mathbb{Z}$, xRy if $xy > 0$

(c) On $\mathbb{Z}^+$, xRy if $xy > 0$

(d) On $\mathbb{Z}$, xRy if $xy \geq 0$

(e) On $\mathbb{R}$, aRb if $|a - b| \leq \frac{1}{2}$

(f) On $\mathbb{R}$, aRb if $z \in \mathbb{Z}$ exists so that $|z - a| \leq \frac{1}{2}$ and $|z - b| \leq \frac{1}{2}$

(g) On the set of lines in a plane, lRm if l is parallel to m

(h) On $\mathbb{R}^2$ $(a,b) R(c,d)$ if $bd = 0$

(i) On the set of triangles, ARB if A is similar to B

(j) On the set of triangles, ARB if A is congruent to B

(k) On the set of lines in a plane, lRm if l is perpendicular to m

3 In $\mathbb{R}^2$, define R by $(a,b) R(c,d)$ if $a - b = c - d$. Show that R is an equivalence relation, and find its equivalence classes.

4 In $\mathbb{R}^2$, define R by $(a,b) R(c,d)$ if $\max(|a|, |b|) = \max(|c|, |d|)$. Show that R is an equivalence relation, find its equivalence classes and describe them geometrically.

5 In $\mathbb{R}^2 \setminus \{(0,0)\}$, define R by $(a,b) R(c,d)$ if $|a| + |b| = |c| + |d|$. Show that R is an equivalence relation, find its equivalence classes and describe them geometrically.

6 In $\mathbb{R}^2$, define R by $(a,b) R(c,d)$ if $a^2 + b^2 = c^2 + d^2$. Show that R is an equivalence relation, find its equivalence classes and describe them geometrically.

3 Functions

This chapter generalises the idea of a function. There is a mass of detail here, some of which you may know already. When you have completed it, you should

- know the meaning of the word 'function' or 'mapping'
- know the language and notation associated with functions
- know the meanings of the terms 'injection', 'surjection' and 'bijection'
- be able to prove whether a given function is an injection, a surjection, a bijection, or none of these
- know what the composition of two functions means, the notation for it, and the conditions under which it exists
- know what an inverse function is, the conditions for the inverse function to exist, and how to find the inverse of a composition of functions
- know that the composition of functions is associative.

Section 3.10 gives an alternative definition of a function which links it to relations. You can omit this if you wish.

3.1 Introduction

You already know a definition of a function, in the context of functions of real numbers and their graphs. So you will see that the definition given in this chapter is a generalisation. If you have already met the generalised idea of a function, then this chapter is likely to be a revision of these ideas, notation and language; in that case, use it mainly for reference.

In some contexts functions are called mappings and the words 'function' and 'mapping' have the same meaning.

3.2 Functions: a discussion

In the context of graphs, people talk about a function of x such as $f(x) = x^2$. But what are the properties that f must have in order to be called a function?

First, what is x? In the case $f(x) = x^2$ there is an understanding that x is a real number, but in the case $g(x) = \sqrt{x}$, the positive square root of x, there is an understanding that x is a positive real number or zero. The point is that in each case x is a member of a starting or object set, although you may not be told explicitly what this starting or object set is. In the generalisation which follows, x will be taken from an object set which will be called the **domain**, and you will be told explicitly what the domain is.

Secondly, what about the result x^2 obtained by operating on x with the function f? It also belongs to a set: this is sometimes called the target set, but more often the **co-domain**. Once again, you should be told explicitly what the co-domain is. In the example $f(x) = x^2$ the co-domain may be $\mathbb{R}$, or it may be $\mathbb{R}^+ \cup \{0\}$. In the context of graphs, you may not be told what the domain is, and often it will not matter precisely what the co-domain is; in this book you will always be told the target set or co-domain.

Thirdly, when you are told that f is a function, you expect that for every value of x you have a rule for calculating the value $f(x)$ of the function corresponding to x. There are two points to emphasise here.

The rule must enable you to calculate the value of $f(x)$ for *every* value of x. And you must be able to calculate *the* value of $f(x)$ for every value of x. Both these aspects are important in the generalised definition of a function. There is a rule which for each value of x in the domain gives you just one value of $f(x)$ in the co-domain. Thus $f(x)$ is called the **image** of x under f.

Fig. 3.1 illustrates these three aspects of the idea of a function. You can see

- the starting set, the domain A
- the target set, the co-domain B
- the rule showing the element $b \in B$
  corresponding to $a \in A$.

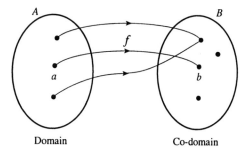

Domain   Co-domain

A function f with domain A and co-domain B

Fig. 3.1

The fact that for each element x in the domain there corresponds just one value of $f(x)$ in the co-domain means that there is exactly one arrow leaving every point in the domain A, with its end in the co-domain B.

Notice that it is not necessary for every element in B to be the image of an element of A.

To summarise:

> A **function** f has three components: a starting set A, called the **domain**; a target set B, called the **co-domain**; and a **rule** which assigns to each member a of A a unique member b of B such that
>
> - every element of A has an associated element of B, and
>
> - no element of A has more than one associated element of B.

There is no reason why A and B should not be the same set.

3.3 Notation and language

You write $f : A \to B$ to show that f is a function for which the domain is A and the co-domain is B.

You say that f maps a to b, and that f maps A into B. The notation to indicate that a maps to b is either $b = f(a)$ or $f : a \mapsto b$.

The set

$$\{b \mid b \in B, b = f(a) \text{ for some } a \in A\}$$

is called the **set of images** or **image set** of A. It is also called the **range** of f.

Two functions $f : A \to B$ and $g : C \to D$ are **equal** if and only if $A = C$, $B = D$ and $f(x) = g(x)$ for every element x in A.

In Fig. 3.2 the image set of A is a subset of B containing just two elements.

A natural extension of the idea of image set that you will meet later in the book is that of the **image of a subset** of A. Let $f:A \rightarrow B$, and let $X \subseteq A$. Then the image $f(X)$ of the subset X is defined by $f(X) = \{f(x) \mid x \in X\}$.

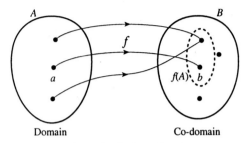

The function $I_A : A \rightarrow A$ given by $I_A(x) = x$ for all $x \in A$ is called the **identity function** on A. If there is no ambiguity, the subscript A can be omitted.

Domain   Co-domain

The image $f(A)$ is shown dotted

Fig. 3.2

Example 3.3.1

For the two examples discussed in Section 3.2, $f(x) = x^2$ and $g(x) = \sqrt{x}$, give complete definitions of f and g.

Possible definitions are

$f : \mathbb{R} \rightarrow \mathbb{R}$ such that $f(x) = x^2$

$g : \mathbb{R}^+ \cup \{0\} \rightarrow \mathbb{R}$ such that $g(x) = \sqrt{x}$, the positive square root of x.

Notice that for both the functions f and g, the set of images is not the same as the whole domain $\mathbb{R}$. You could have defined the function f differently by saying that

$f : \mathbb{R} \rightarrow \mathbb{R}^+ \cup \{0\}$ such that $f(x) = x^2$

but in that case, the two functions called f are different. This illustrates an important fact: that to be equal, two functions must have the same domain, the same co-domain and the same rule.

> Two functions f and g are **equal** if, and only if, they have the same domain, the same co-domain and the same rule.

Example 3.3.2

Explain why $f : \mathbb{Q} \rightarrow \mathbb{Z}$ defined by $f(x) =$ the numerator of the fraction x is not a function.

This example fails the uniqueness part of the definition of a function as $f\left(\frac{1}{2}\right) = 1$ and $f\left(\frac{2}{4}\right) = 2$.

Example 3.3.3

Explain why $f : \mathbb{Z} \rightarrow \mathbb{Q}$ given by $f(n) = \dfrac{1}{n}$ is not a function.

The function $f(n)$ is not defined for $n = 0$.

Example 3.3.4

Let $X =$ set of times on a specified day, and $Y =$ set of trains leaving Victoria Station in London on that day. Then let $f : X \rightarrow Y$ be given by $f(x) =$ train leaving Victoria Station at time x. Explain why f is not a function.

This example fails on two grounds: given a particular time, there may not be a train leaving Victoria Station at that time; and there may be some times at which more than one train leaves Victoria Station.

3.4   Injections and surjections

A function $f : A \rightarrow B$ is called an **injection** if each element of B has at most one element of A mapped into it. The adjective **injective** is used to describe a function which is an injection. An injection is also called a **one-to-one function**.

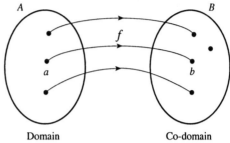

Domain   Co-domain
An injection: no two arrows go to the same element in B

Fig. 3.3

Fig. 3.3 illustrates an injection. Each element of B has at most one arrow coming into it from an element of A. Notice that there may be elements of B which are not images of elements of A.

Proving that a given function f is an injection is equivalent to proving that if $f(a) = f(b)$ then $a = b$. Simply writing down $f(a) = f(b)$ as the first line is often a good way to start the proof. Example 3.4.1 illustrates this.

A function $f : A \rightarrow B$ is called a **surjection** if each element of B has at least one member of A mapped into it, that is, the range of f is the whole of the co-domain. The adjective **surjective** is used to describe a function which is a surjection. A surjection is also called an **onto function**.

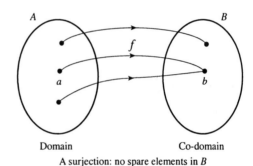

Domain   Co-domain
A surjection: no spare elements in B

Fig. 3.4

Fig. 3.4 illustrates a surjection. Each element of B has at least one arrow coming into it from an element in A. Some elements in B may be the image of more than one element in A.

A function $f : A \rightarrow B$ which is both an injection and a surjection is called a **bijection**. The adjective **bijective** is used to describe a function which is a bijection. A bijection is also called a **one-to-one correspondence**.

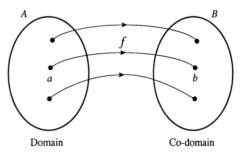

Domain   Co-domain
A bijection: both an injection and a surjection

Fig. 3.5

Fig. 3.5 illustrates a bijection. Each element of B has exactly one arrow coming into it from an element of A.

Example 3.4.1
Prove that the function $f : \mathbb{Z} \to \mathbb{Z}$ such that $f(n) = n + 1$ is both an injection and a surjection.

To prove that f is an injection, suppose that two elements a and b map to the same image under f. Then $f(a) = f(b)$ so $a + 1 = b + 1$, leading to $a = b$.

This method is one you will often use for proving that a function is an injection. Start by supposing that two different elements have identical images, and then show that the elements themselves must be identical.

To prove that f is a surjection, you must find the element in the domain which maps onto any given element in the co-domain. So if you take an element n in the co-domain, consider the element $n - 1$ in the domain. Then $f(n-1) = (n-1) + 1 = n$. So every element n in the co-domain has a corresponding element $n - 1$ in the domain.

This method is fairly typical for proving that a function f is a surjection. For any given element of the co-domain, you have to identify an element in the domain which maps onto it.

In Example 3.4.1, as f is both an injection and a surjection, f is a bijection.

Example 3.4.2
Show that the projection function $p : \mathbb{R}^2 \to \mathbb{R}^2$ defined by $p(x, y) = (x, 0)$ is neither an injection nor a surjection.

To prove that p is not an injection, you need to find two elements in the domain which have the same image under p. Since $p(0,1) = (0,0)$ and $p(0,0) = (0,0)$, p is not an injection.

To prove that p is not a surjection, you need to find an element in the co-domain $\mathbb{R}^2$ which is not the image of any element of the domain $\mathbb{R}^2$. Consider the element $(0,1)$ and suppose it is the image of (x, y). Then $p(x, y) = (x, 0) = (0,1)$, which implies that $x = 0$ and $0 = 1$. As the second of these is impossible, no such element exists, and p is not a surjection.

3.5 Injections and surjections of finite sets

Here are two theorems about surjective and injective functions when the domain and co-domain are finite sets.

You may find it useful to draw diagrams like Figs. 3.3 to 3.5 to illustrate the theorems for yourself. The results may then appear to be obvious.

Before the theorems, here is a reminder about notation. If X is a finite set then $n(X)$ means the number of elements in X. Similarly, $n(f(X))$ means the number of elements in $f(X)$.

Theorem 3.1   Let X and Y be finite sets, and let $f : X \to Y$ be a function. Then

(a) $n(f(X)) \le n(X)$

(b) f is injective if, and only if, $n(f(X)) = n(X)$

(c) f is surjective if, and only if, $n(f(X)) = n(Y)$.

  (a) **Proof**

By the definition of function, to each $x \in X$ there is assigned one, and only one, element of Y. So to each element of $f(X)$, there corresponds at least one element of X; and no two different elements of $f(X)$ are associated with the same element of X. Therefore $n(f(X)) \le n(X)$.

(b)   **Proof of 'if'**
Suppose that $n(f(X)) = n(X)$. Then X and $f(X)$ have the same number of elements. Suppose that $f(x_1) = f(x_2)$ for $x_1, x_2 \in X$. If $x_1 \ne x_2$, then $n(f(X)) \le n(X)$, since the images of two different elements in X would be the same. But as $n(f(X)) = n(X)$, $x_1 = x_2$, and f is an injection.

Proof of 'only if'
Suppose that f is injective. Then, if $f(x_1) = f(x_2)$, $x_1 = x_2$. Therefore the elements of $f(X)$ are all different, and $n(f(X)) = n(X)$.

(c)   **Proof of 'if'**
Suppose that $n(f(X)) = n(Y)$. Then $f(X)$ and Y have the same number of elements. But $f(X) \subseteq Y$. Therefore $f(X) = Y$. Therefore every element of Y is the image of some member $x \in X$. Therefore f is a surjection.

Proof of 'only if'
Suppose that f is surjective. Then every element of Y is the image of some element of X. So $Y \subseteq f(X)$. But $f(X) \subseteq Y$. Therefore $f(X) = Y$, so $n(f(X)) = n(Y)$.

Since, by definition, $f(X) \subseteq Y$, and so $n(f(X)) \le n(Y)$, you can deduce that if f is an injection, $n(X) \le n(Y)$. Or, put an equivalent way, if $n(X) > n(Y)$, then f is not an injection.

This is the **pigeon-hole principle**. It is stated in the following way, with the justification in brackets.

Suppose that you have pigeons which are put into pigeon-holes (that is, a function $f : X \to Y$), and you have more pigeons than pigeon-holes (that is, $n(X) > n(Y)$), then there is at least one pigeon-hole with more than one pigeon (that is, f is not injective).

The pigeon-hole principle has some quite surprising applications. Here is a none-too-serious example.

Example 3.5.1
Let $X =$ the set of non-bald people in England, and let $Y =$ the set of positive integers less than a million. Let $f : X \to Y$ be given by $f(x) =$ the number of hairs on the head of x. Prove that there are at least two people in England with the same number of hairs on their heads.

It is a fact that no-one has more than a million hairs on his or her head, (the number is usually 150 000 to 200 000), so f is well defined.

It is also a fact that $n(X) > n(Y)$, that is, the number of non-bald people in England is greater than a million.

It follows from the pigeon-hole principle that f is not injective, and hence that there are at least two people in England with the same number of hairs on their heads.

Theorem 3.2   Let X and Y be finite sets, let $n(X) = n(Y)$, and let $f : X \rightarrow Y$ be a function. Then f is injective if, and only if, f is surjective.

Proof of 'if'
Suppose that f is surjective. Then, by Theorem 3.1(c), $n(f(X)) = n(Y)$. But, by hypothesis, $n(X) = n(Y)$, so $n(f(X)) = n(X)$. Therefore, by Theorem 3.1(b), f is injective.

Proof of 'only if'
Suppose that f is injective. Then, by Theorem 3.1(b), $n(f(X)) = n(X)$. But, by hypothesis, $n(X) = n(Y)$, so $n(f(X)) = n(Y)$. Then, by Theorem 3.1(c), f is surjective.

Exercise 3A

1   Prove that $f : \mathbb{R} \rightarrow \mathbb{R}$ defined by $f(x) = \sin x$ is neither an injection nor a surjection.

2   Give an example of a function $f : \mathbb{R} \rightarrow \mathbb{R}$ which is an injection, but not a surjection.

3   Give an example of a function $f : \mathbb{R} \rightarrow \mathbb{R}$ which is a surjection, but not an injection.

4   In each of these examples the domain is $\mathbb{R}$ and the co-domain is $\mathbb{R}$. Decide which of them is the definition of a function. If it is a function, decide whether it is injective, and whether it is surjective. Be able to justify your answers. Keep your answers: they will be used in Exercise 3B Question 3.

 (a) $f(x) = x^2$ (b) $f(x) = x^3$ (c) $f(x) = 1/x$ (d) $f(x) = \cos x$
 (e) $f(x) = \tan x$ (f) $f(x) = e^x$ (g) $f(x) = |x|$ (h) $f(x) = \sqrt{x}$
 (i) $f(x) = x + 1$ (j) $f(x) = \text{int } x$ (int x is the largest integer $\leq x$.)
 (k) $f(x) = \sin^{-1} x$ (l) $f(x)$ is the smallest real number greater than x.

5   Prove that the function $f : \mathbb{R}^+ \cup \{0\} \rightarrow \mathbb{R}^+ \cup \{0\}$ defined by $f(x) = \sqrt{x}$ is a bijection.

6   Prove that the function $f : \mathbb{R} \setminus \{0\} \rightarrow \mathbb{R} \setminus \{0\}$ defined by $f(x) = 1/x$ is a bijection.

7   Prove that the function $f : \mathbb{Z} \rightarrow \mathbb{Z}^+$ defined by $f(n) = \begin{cases} 2n, & \text{if } n > 0 \\ 1 - 2n, & \text{if } n \leq 0 \end{cases}$ is a bijection.

8   How can you tell from the graph of a real function $y = f(x)$, whether or not f is

 (a) an injection,   (b) a surjection,   (c) a bijection?

9   Mark each of the following statements true or false.

 (a) The function $f : \mathbb{R} \rightarrow \mathbb{R}$ such that $f(x) = 0$ for all $x \in \mathbb{R}$, is a bijection.
 (b) Every function which is a bijection is also a surjection.
 (c) $f : \mathbb{R} \times \mathbb{R} \rightarrow \mathbb{R} \times \mathbb{R}$ defined by $f(x, y) = (y, x)$, is a bijection.

10   Let $P = \{\text{polynomials in } x \text{ with real coefficients}\}$. Decide whether $f : P \rightarrow P$ defined in the following ways is a function. If it is, decide whether it is injective, and whether it is surjective.

 (a) $f(p) = \dfrac{d(p(x))}{dx}$ (b) $f(p) = \displaystyle\int p(t)\, dt$ (c) $f(p) = \displaystyle\int_0^x p(t)\, dt$ (d) $f(p) = xp(x)$

3.6 Combining functions

When the co-domain of one function is the domain of another function you can combine the two functions in the way indicated by Fig. 3.6.

In Fig. 3.6, $b = f(a)$ and $c = g(b)$. The composite function is the function which maps a from the set A directly to c in set C.

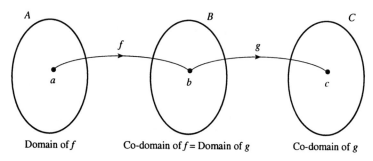

Fig. 3.6

But first you have to establish that the rule which takes a to c is actually a properly defined function.

Theorem 3.3   Let $f : A \to B$ and $g : B \to C$ be functions. Then $h : A \to C$ such that $h(x) = g(f(x))$ is a function.

Proof

To show that h is a function, you need to exhibit its domain and its co-domain, and to show that for every element in the domain there is a unique element in the co-domain.

In this case the domain is A, and the co-domain is C, so it only remains to show the existence and uniqueness properties.

For each element $a \in A$ there exists a unique element $f(a) = b$ in B. Moreover, for that $b \in B$ there is a unique element $g(b) = c$ in C. It follows that for each element $a \in A$ there exists a unique element $c \in C$,, such that $c = g(f(a))$.

This shows that $h : A \to C$ such that $h(x) = g(f(x))$ is a function.

Let $f : A \to B$ and $g : B \to C$ be functions.

Then the function $h : A \to C$ such that $h(x) = g(f(x))$ is called the **composite** of f and g, written sometimes as $g \circ f$ and sometimes as gf.

Then $(g \circ f)(x) = g(f(x))$.

The composite function $g \circ f$ is pronounced 'g blob f'.

Notice that for the composite function to be properly defined it is not necessary that the function $f : A \to B$ is a surjection. For example, let $f : \mathbb{R} \to \mathbb{R}$ be given by $f(x) = \sin x$ and $g : \mathbb{R} \to \mathbb{R}$ be given by $g(x) = 2x$. Then the function $(g \circ f) : \mathbb{R} \to \mathbb{R}$ is defined by $(g \circ f)(x) = g(f(x)) = 2\sin x$, even though the image set of f is the set $\{x \mid x \in \mathbb{R}, -1 \le x \le 1\}$ and not the whole of $\mathbb{R}$.

Example 3.6.1

Let $f : \mathbb{R} \to \mathbb{R}$ where $f(x) = 2x + 1$ and $g : \mathbb{R} \to \mathbb{R}$ where $g(x) = 2x$. Show that $fg \neq gf$.

To show that two functions are not equal, you do not need a general argument. You only need to find a single value of x for which $fg(x) \neq gf(x)$.

For this case,

$$fg(1) = f(2) = 5 \qquad \text{and} \qquad gf(1) = g(3) = 6.$$

Hence $fg \neq gf$.

> Let $f : A \to A$ and $g : A \to A$ be functions.
>
> Then the functions $fg : A \to A$ and $gf : A \to A$ are not usually equal.

Note that there may be cases when $fg = gf$, but these are exceptions. In general, $fg \neq gf$.

What can you deduce about the composite function $(g \circ f) : A \to C$ when you know some of the properties of the functions $f : A \to B$ and $g : B \to C$? For example, if f and g are both surjections, will $g \circ f$ be a surjection?

The answer is yes. The result itself is not important, but the method of proof is important. As in all proofs about surjections, you have to find an element in A which maps to a given element in the image C.

Example 3.6.2

Prove that if $f : A \to B$ and $g : B \to C$ are surjections, then $(g \circ f) : A \to C$ is also a surjection.

Notice that the conditions for a composite function are satisfied, so the composite function $(g \circ f) : A \to C$ exists.

Now suppose that c is any element in C. Then, since g is surjective, there exists an element $b \in B$ such that $g(b) = c$; and as f is surjective, there exists an element $a \in A$ such that $f(a) = b$. Thus $(g \circ f)(a) = g(f(a)) = g(b) = c$. So $(g \circ f) : A \to C$ is a surjection.

Example 3.6.3

Suppose that $f : A \to B$ is an injection and $g : B \to C$ is a surjection. Can you deduce that
(a) the function $(g \circ f) : A \to C$ is a surjection,   (b) the function $(g \circ f) : A \to C$ is an injection?

(a)   You cannot deduce that $(g \circ f) : A \to C$ is a surjection.

For let $f : \{a,b\} \to \{p,q,r\}$ be given by $f(a) = p$ and $f(b) = q$. Then f is an injection.

And let $g : \{p,q,r\} \to \{s,t\}$ where $g(p) = g(q) = s$ and $g(r) = t$. Then g is a surjection.

Now, $(g \circ f) : \{a,b\} \to \{s,t\}$ is given by $(g \circ f)(a) = s$ and $(g \circ f)(b) = s$. So there is no $x \in A$ such that $(g \circ f)(x) = t$, so $(g \circ f) : A \to C$ is not a surjection.

(b)   Also $(g \circ f): A \to C$ is not an injection, because a and b are distinct elements of A mapping to the element s in C under $g \circ f$.

This section ends with a proof of an obvious-looking theorem involving the identity function.

Theorem 3.3   For any function $f: A \to A$, $I_A \circ f = f = f \circ I_A$.

Proof

For $a \in A$, $(I_A \circ f)(a) = I_A(f(a)) = f(a)$.

Also $(f \circ I_A)(a) = f(I_A(a)) = f(a)$.

It follows that $I_A \circ f = f = f \circ I_A$.

3.7   Inverse functions

Here is an important question about functions. Suppose that $f: A \to B$ is a function. Under what circumstances is there a reverse function g from B to A which has the opposite effect to f? That is, under what conditions does there exist a function $g: B \to A$ such that $g(b) = a$ whenever $f(a) = b$?

The answer is that there will be a function $g: B \to A$ which reverses the effect of $f: A \to B$, if, and only if, $f: A \to B$ is a bijection.

Proving this apparently straightforward statement is long and detailed. If it would make you feel more comfortable, jump to the end of the section, and come back to study the details later.

Theorem 3.4 $f: A \to B$ is a bijection if, and only if, there exists a function $g: B \to A$ with $g(f(a)) = a$ for all $a \in A$, and $f(g(b)) = b$ for all $b \in B$.

Proof

Consider the following two statements.

(a)   There exists a function $g: B \to A$ such that $g(f(a)) = a$ for all $a \in A$, and $f(g(b)) = b$ for all $b \in B$.

(b) $f: A \to B$ is a bijection.

The proof comes in two stages. The first stage is to show that if statement (a) is true, then statement (b) is true. Thus you need to show that f is injective and surjective.

Suppose that statement (a) is true.

Proof that f is an injection
If $f(x) = f(y)$, then $g(f(x)) = g(f(y))$, so, by the first part of the hypothesis of statement (a), $x = y$. Hence $f: A \to B$ is injective.

Proof that f is a surjection
If $b \in B$, then, from the second part of the hypothesis of statement (a), $b = f(g(b))$ is the image under f of $g(b) \in A$. Hence $f: A \to B$ is surjective.

Hence $f: A \to B$ is both injective and surjective, so it is bijective.

The second stage consists of showing that if statement (b) is true, then statement (a) is true. The first part of this stage consists of showing that the function g is well-defined.

Now suppose that statement (b) is true, that is, $f : A \rightarrow B$ is a bijection.

Proof that g is well-defined

As $f : A \rightarrow B$ is a bijection, for every $b \in B$, there is at least one $a \in A$ such that $f(a) = b$ because f is surjective. But, given b, there cannot be more than one $a \in A$ such that $f(a) = b$ because f is injective. Therefore, specifying $g(b)$ to be that unique $a \in A$ such that $f(a) = b$ gives a well-defined function $g : B \rightarrow A$.

So g is well defined. Now you have to show that the function g has the required properties in (a).

For $b \in B$, $f(g(b)) = f(a) = b$.

Also, for $a \in A$, if you write $b = f(a)$, then $g(b)$ is, by definition, equal to a, so $g(f(a)) = a$.

The theorem tells you that $f : A \rightarrow B$ is a bijection if, and only if, there is a function $g : B \rightarrow A$ such that $g \circ f = I_A$ and $f \circ g = I_B$. And now, from this, you can define an inverse function.

The function $g : B \rightarrow A$ of the previous theorem is called an **inverse** of f.

There are still two more results to prove in this section. These results are the two parts of Theorem 3.5.

Theorem 3.5   Let $f : A \rightarrow B$ be a bijection. Then the function $g : B \rightarrow A$ with $g(f(a)) = a$, for all $a \in A$, and $b = f(g(b))$, for all $b \in B$ is

(a) a bijection,

(b) uniquely determined by f.

Proof

The function f plays the role of an inverse for g, so the previous theorem can be applied to g. This shows that g is a bijection.

Remember in proving part (b), uniqueness, that two functions are equal if they have the same domain, co-domain, and have the same effect on every element of the domain.

To prove the uniqueness, suppose that $g : B \rightarrow A$ and $h : B \rightarrow A$ are both inverses of f. Then $f(g(b)) = b = f(h(b))$ for all $b \in B$. Therefore, since f is injective, $g(b) = h(b)$ for all $b \in B$. Therefore $g = h$.

You can now talk about *the* inverse f^{-1} (rather than *an* inverse) of a bijection $f : A \rightarrow B$. This is the function $f^{-1} : B \rightarrow A$ such that $f \circ f^{-1} = I_B$ and $f^{-1} \circ f = I_A$.

Let $f : A \rightarrow B$ be a bijection.

Then the function $g : B \rightarrow A$ with $g(f(a)) = a$, for all $a \in A$, and $b = f(g(b))$, for all $b \in B$ is a bijection, and is called the **inverse** of f.

The inverse of f is written as f^{-1}.

3.8 Associativity of functions

Suppose that $f:A \to B$, $g:B \to C$ and $h:C \to D$ are three functions. Then you can combine them to form composite functions in two ways: you could combine f and g first to get $g \circ f$ and then combine this with h to get the function $(h \circ (g \circ f)) : A \to D$; or you could work the other way round to get $((h \circ g) \circ f) : A \to D$. You probably suspect that it doesn't matter which way you write it – the result will be the same. You are right!

To prove it, you need to go back to the definitions in Section 3.6.

Theorem 3.6   Let $f:A \to B$, $g:B \to C$ and $h:C \to D$ be functions. Then $(h \circ g) \circ f = h \circ (g \circ f)$.

Proof

Using the definition of composite function on $((h \circ g) \circ f)(x)$ gives

$$((h \circ g) \circ f)(x) = (h \circ g)(f(x)) = h(g(f(x))).$$

Also $(h \circ (g \circ f))(x)$ gives

$$(h \circ (g \circ f))(x) = h((g \circ f)(x)) = h(g(f(x))).$$

As the domains and co-domains of $(h \circ g) \circ f$ and $h \circ (g \circ f)$ are the same and $((h \circ g) \circ f)(x) = (h \circ (g \circ f))(x)$ for any x in A, it follows that the functions $(h \circ g) \circ f$ and $h \circ (g \circ f)$ are equal.

It is also easy to see, but tedious to write out a proof, that a kind of generalised associative law holds for composite functions. If p, q, r and s are four functions with compatible domains and co-domains so that they can be composed together, you can talk about the function $s \circ r \circ q \circ p$ without brackets.

3.9 Inverse of a composite function

It is useful now to introduce a collapsed form of the usual diagram for sets and functions. Let $f : A \to B$ and $g : B \to C$ be functions. These functions are illustrated in Fig. 3.7, together with $g \circ f : A \to C$.

Now suppose that the functions $f : A \to B$ and $g : B \to C$ are both bijections, so that the inverse functions $f^{-1} : B \to A$ and $g^{-1} : C \to B$ both exist. What can you say about the inverse of the composite function $(g \circ f) : A \to C$? Fig. 3.8 helps to make the situation clear.

From Fig. 3.8 you can surmise that the inverse of the function $g \circ f$ is $f^{-1} \circ g^{-1}$. This is proved in the next theorem (Theorem 3.7).

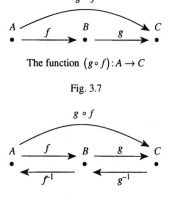

The function $(g \circ f) : A \to C$

Fig. 3.7

The inverse of $(g \circ f) : A \to C$

Fig. 3.8

To prove this result you need to go back to Theorem 3.5 and check the details of the theorem are satisfied. You need to check that $(f^{-1} \circ g^{-1}) \circ (g \circ f) = I_A$ and $(g \circ f) \circ (f^{-1} \circ g^{-1}) = I_C$.

Theorem 3.7   Let the two functions $f : A \rightarrow B$ and $g : B \rightarrow C$ be bijections. Then the inverse of the function $(g \circ f) : A \rightarrow C$ exists and is the function $\left(f^{-1} \circ g^{-1}\right) : C \rightarrow A$. Furthermore $g \circ f$ and $f^{-1} \circ g^{-1}$ are both bijections.

Proof
You need to show that $\left(f^{-1} \circ g^{-1}\right) \circ (g \circ f) = I_A$. Then you need to show that $(g \circ f) \circ \left(f^{-1} \circ g^{-1}\right) = I_C$.

For the first part,

$$\left(f^{-1} \circ g^{-1}\right) \circ (g \circ f) = f^{-1} \circ \left(g^{-1} \circ (g \circ f)\right)$$
$$= f^{-1} \circ \left(\left(g^{-1} \circ g\right) \circ f\right)$$
$$= f^{-1} \circ \left(I_B \circ f\right)$$
$$= f^{-1} \circ f \qquad \text{(using Theorem 3.3)}$$
$$= I_A.$$

Secondly,

$$(g \circ f) \circ \left(f^{-1} \circ g^{-1}\right) = g \circ \left(f \circ \left(f^{-1} \circ g^{-1}\right)\right)$$
$$= g \circ \left(\left(f \circ f^{-1}\right) \circ g^{-1}\right)$$
$$= g \circ \left(I_B \circ g^{-1}\right)$$
$$= g \circ g^{-1} \qquad \text{(using Theorem 3.3)}$$
$$= I_C.$$

Therefore $f^{-1} \circ g^{-1}$ is the inverse of $g \circ f$.

Also it follows from Theorem 3.4 that $g \circ f$ and $f^{-1} \circ g^{-1}$ are bijections.

You can think of Theorem 3.7 in terms of doing and un-doing certain actions. For example, if you want to reverse the effect of putting on your socks and then putting on your climbing boots, you would first take off your boots and then take off your socks.

Example 3.9.1
Let $f : \mathbb{R} \rightarrow \mathbb{R}$ where $f(x) = 2x + 1$ and $g : \mathbb{R} \rightarrow \mathbb{R}$ where $g(x) = 2x$. Assuming that f and g are bijections,
(a) write down the inverses of f and g,
(b) hence find the inverses of $g \circ f$ and $f \circ g$.

(a)   The inverse of f is given by $f^{-1}(x) = \frac{1}{2}(x - 1)$, and the inverse of g is given by $g^{-1}(x) = \frac{1}{2}x$.

(b)   The inverse of $g \circ f$ is $f^{-1} \circ g^{-1}$, so

$$(g \circ f)^{-1}(x) = \left(f^{-1} \circ g^{-1}\right)(x)$$
$$= f^{-1}\left(g^{-1}(x)\right)$$
$$= f^{-1}\left(\tfrac{1}{2}x\right)$$
$$= \tfrac{1}{2}\left(\tfrac{1}{2}x - 1\right)$$
$$= \tfrac{1}{4}x - \tfrac{1}{2}$$

and

$$(f \circ g)^{-1}(x) = \left(g^{-1} \circ f^{-1}\right)(x)$$
$$= g^{-1}\left(f^{-1}(x)\right)$$
$$= g^{-1}\left(\tfrac{1}{2}(x - 1)\right)$$
$$= \tfrac{1}{2}\left(\tfrac{1}{2}(x - 1)\right)$$
$$= \tfrac{1}{4}x - \tfrac{1}{4}.$$

3.10 Functions: an alternative definition

You may omit this section if you wish.

If you look back at the definition of a function in Section 3.2, it mentions a domain, a co-domain and a rule. Some people say that the word 'rule' is not defined. In fact, a rule is hard to define, so here is an alternative way of thinking about functions which gets around this point. You will find this alternative approach in some books.

Let A and B be two sets. A function f which has A as its domain and B as its co-domain is a subset of $A \times B$ with the following properties:

- every $a \in A$ is the first coordinate of some $(a,b) \in f$
- if (a,b_1) and $(a,b_2) \in f$, then $b_1 = b_2$.

You can see, if you think about it, that this definition agrees with the one in Section 3.2, and that it gets round the difficulty of knowing what a rule is. However, you have used functions for some time, so presumably you recognise a rule when you see one, and there is not really a good case for changing the emphasis now.

Exercise 3B

1   Prove that, if $f : A \to B$ and $g : B \to A$ are such that $g \circ f = I_A$, then f is an injection and g is a surjection.

2   Let $f : \mathbb{R} \to \mathbb{R}$ be given by $f(x) = x^2 + 1$. Decide whether or not f is

   (a) surjective,   (b) injective,   (c) bijective.

3   In Question 2 of Exercise 3A you decided whether each of the following definitions was the definition of a function and, if so, whether it was injective and whether it was surjective. Use your answer to decide which of the functions have inverses, and give inverses for these functions.

(a) $f(x) = x^2$

(b) $f(x) = x^3$

(c) $f(x) = 1/x$

(d) $f(x) = \cos x$

(e) $f(x) = \tan x$

(f) $f(x) = e^x$

(g) $f(x) = |x|$

(h) $f(x) = \sqrt{x}$

(i) $f(x) = x + 1$

(j) $f(x) = \operatorname{int} x$ ($\operatorname{int} x$ is the largest integer $\leq x$.)

(k) $f(x) = \sin^{-1} x$

(l) $f(x)$ is the smallest real number greater than x .

4   Show that the function $g : \mathbb{Z}^+ \to \mathbb{Z}$ defined by

$$g(n) = \begin{cases} n/2, \text{ if } n \text{ is even} \\ (1-n)/2, \text{ if } n \text{ is odd} \end{cases}$$

is inverse to the function $f : \mathbb{Z} \to \mathbb{Z}^+$ of Question 7 in Exercise 3A.

5   Mark each of the following statements true or false. Justify your answers.

(a) The inverse of $f \circ g$ is $f^{-1} \circ g^{-1}$.

(b) If f is a bijection, then f is an injection.

(c) An injection is a bijection if, and only if, it is a surjection.

(d) An injection from a finite set to itself is also a surjection.

(e) An injection from an infinite set to itself is also a surjection.

(f) If $g \circ f$ is a bijection and f is a bijection, then g is a bijection.

(g) If $g \circ f$ is an injection and g is a injection, then f is a injection.

6   Let a function $f(x)$ be defined for all values of $\mathbb{R}$. Prove that the relation xRy defined by xRy if, and only if, $f(x) = f(y)$, is an equivalence relation, and find the equivalence classes. In particular, find the equivalence classes for the function $f(x) = \sin 2x$ for the case when $\left\{ x \mid x \in \mathbb{R}, f(x) = \dfrac{1}{\sqrt{2}} \right\}$.

7   Let $f : \mathbb{R} \to \mathbb{R}$ be given by $f(x) = \frac{1}{2}x + 1$, and $g : \mathbb{R} \to \mathbb{R}^+$ be given by $g(x) = e^x$.

(a) Show that f and g are both bijections.

(b) Write down the inverses of f and g .

(c) Use the results of part (b) to find the inverse of the real function h where $h(x) = e^{\frac{1}{2}x+1}$.

8   Show that the function $f : \mathbb{R}^2 \to \mathbb{R}^2$ given by $f(x, y) = (3x + 2y, 5x + 4y)$ is

(a) a surjection,

(b) an injection,

and find an expression for its inverse.

9 Investigate whether the functions $f : \mathbb{R}^2 \to \mathbb{R}^2$ and $g : \mathbb{R}^2 \to \mathbb{R}^2$ defined by

$$f\begin{pmatrix} x \\ y \end{pmatrix} = \begin{pmatrix} 2 & 1 \\ 0 & 1 \end{pmatrix}\begin{pmatrix} x \\ y \end{pmatrix} \quad \text{and} \quad g\begin{pmatrix} x \\ y \end{pmatrix} = \begin{pmatrix} 1 & -2 \\ -2 & 4 \end{pmatrix}\begin{pmatrix} x \\ y \end{pmatrix}$$

are

(a) injective,   (b) surjective,   (c) bijective.

10 For which value of k is the function $f : \mathbb{R}^3 \to \mathbb{R}^3$ defined by

$$f\begin{pmatrix} x \\ y \\ z \end{pmatrix} = \begin{pmatrix} 1 & 2 & -1 \\ 2 & 3 & -2 \\ 1 & 1 & k \end{pmatrix}\begin{pmatrix} x \\ y \\ z \end{pmatrix}$$

(a) injective,   (b) surjective,   (c) bijective?

4 Binary operations and groups

This chapter introduces and develops the ideas of a set with a binary operation and a group. When you have completed it, you should

- know what a binary operation is
- know the axioms for a group
- know how to decide whether a given structure is, or is not, a group.

4.1 Binary operations

Most of the sets you have met so far have had, in addition to the set of elements, an operation: for example, real numbers and the operation of multiplication.

Multiplication of two real numbers is an example of a **binary operation**; another binary operation is the dot product $a \cdot b$ of two vectors a and b.

> A **binary operation** $\circ$ on a set S is a rule which assigns to each ordered pair of elements x, y in S exactly one element denoted by $x \circ y$.

The binary operation $\circ$ is often pronounced 'blob'!

Notice that multiplication, addition and subtraction are binary operations on $\mathbb{Z}$. On the other hand division is not, since $x \div 0$ has no meaning. Multiplication, addition and subtraction are binary operations on $\mathbb{R}$, $\mathbb{C}$ and $\mathbb{Q}$, but division is not, because you cannot divide by zero.

However, if you use the notation $A \setminus B$ to mean the set which consists of elements of A which are not elements of B, that is,

$$A \setminus B = \{x \mid x \in A \text{ and } x \notin B\},$$

you can then say that division is a binary operation on $\mathbb{R} \setminus \{0\}$, $\mathbb{C} \setminus \{0\}$ and $\mathbb{Q} \setminus \{0\}$.

In the definition of binary operation, notice that $x \circ y$ does not have to be an element of the set S. For example, the scalar product of two vectors is not a vector. However, in cases where the binary operation on S always gives a result which is in the set S, the operation is said to be **closed** within the set.

In some books, the term 'binary operation' is used to mean a closed binary operation.

Example 4.1.1
Decide which of the following operations on the given sets are binary operations. For those which are binary operations, say whether or not they are closed.
(a) $\mathbb{N}$, where $a \circ b$ means $a - b$
(b) $\mathbb{N} \setminus \{0\}$, where $a \circ b$ means the lowest common multiple (lcm) of a and b
(c) $\mathbb{R}$, where $a \circ b$ means the greater of a and b
(d) $\mathbb{R}$, where $a \circ b = \dfrac{a + b}{1 - ab}$

(e) $\mathbb{Z}$, where $a \circ b$ means a

(f) $\mathbb{R}^2$, where $(a,b) \circ (c,d) = (ac - bd, ad + bc)$

    (a)   A binary operation. Since, for example, $1 - 2$ is not defined in $\mathbb{N}$, the operation is not closed.

    (b)   A binary operation. The lowest common multiple (lcm) of two positive integers a and b is always defined. As the lcm is a positive integer, the operation is closed.

    (c)   A binary operation. The greater of a and b is defined, except when $a = b$ when it is understood that $a \circ b$ is equal to either a or b. It is closed since the result is in $\mathbb{R}$.

    (d)   Not a binary operation, since you cannot calculate $1 \circ 1$.

    (e)   A binary operation. As a is in $\mathbb{Z}$ the result $a \circ b = a$ is also in $\mathbb{Z}$, so the binary operation is closed.

    (f)   A binary operation. As $ac - bd$ and $ad + bc$ are both in $\mathbb{R}$, $(ac - bd, ad + bc) \in \mathbb{R}^2$, so the binary operation is closed.

In Example 4.1.1 operations (b) and (c), the order in which a and b are written does not matter since $a \circ b = b \circ a$, but in operations (a) and (e) the order does matter.

> A binary operation $\circ$ on a set S is **commutative** if $a \circ b = b \circ a$ for all $a, b \in S$; otherwise it is **not commutative**.

Important examples of non-commutative binary operations are

- division on $\mathbb{R} \setminus \{0\}$; a counterexample is $2 \div 1 = 2$ and $1 \div 2 = \frac{1}{2}$
- subtraction on $\mathbb{R}$; a counterexample is $3 - 2 = 1$ and $2 - 3 = -1$
- the multiplication of square matrices; a counterexample is $\begin{pmatrix} 1 & 0 \\ 1 & 0 \end{pmatrix}\begin{pmatrix} 0 & 1 \\ 0 & 1 \end{pmatrix} = \begin{pmatrix} 0 & 1 \\ 0 & 1 \end{pmatrix}$ and

$$\begin{pmatrix} 0 & 1 \\ 0 & 1 \end{pmatrix}\begin{pmatrix} 1 & 0 \\ 1 & 0 \end{pmatrix} = \begin{pmatrix} 1 & 0 \\ 1 & 0 \end{pmatrix}.$$

If you have expressions of the form $(a \circ b) \circ c$ and $a \circ (b \circ c)$ where $\circ$ is a closed binary operation and $a, b, c \in S$, it may or may not be true that $(a \circ b) \circ c = a \circ (b \circ c)$. For example, for the binary operation $+$ on $\mathbb{R}$, you can say that $(a + b) + c = a + (b + c)$, but for the binary operation $-$ on $\mathbb{R}$, the counterexample $(4 - 2) - 1 = 1$ and $4 - (2 - 1) = 3$; shows that in general, $(a - b) - c \neq a - (b - c)$.

> A closed binary operation $\circ$ on a set S is **associative** if $(a \circ b) \circ c = a \circ (b \circ c)$ for all $a, b, c \in S$; otherwise it is **not associative**.

When a binary operation is associative, you may leave out the brackets and write $a \circ b \circ c$, since both ways of evaluating it give the same answer.

Example 4.1.2

Say whether or not the following closed binary operations are commutative and associative.

(a) $\mathbb{N}$: multiplication

(b) Matrices of the form $\begin{pmatrix} x & x \\ 0 & 0 \end{pmatrix}$, where $x \in \mathbb{R}$: matrix multiplication

(c) Vectors in three dimensions: vector product

(d) $\mathbb{Z}$: the operation $a \circ b$ defined as $a + b - ab$

(a)   For natural numbers $ab = ba$ and $(ab)c = a(bc)$, so the operation is commutative and associative.

(b) $\begin{pmatrix} x & x \\ 0 & 0 \end{pmatrix}\begin{pmatrix} y & y \\ 0 & 0 \end{pmatrix} = \begin{pmatrix} xy & xy \\ 0 & 0 \end{pmatrix}$ and $\begin{pmatrix} y & y \\ 0 & 0 \end{pmatrix}\begin{pmatrix} x & x \\ 0 & 0 \end{pmatrix} = \begin{pmatrix} yx & yx \\ 0 & 0 \end{pmatrix}$. As $x, y \in \mathbb{R}$, $xy = yx$, and

$\begin{pmatrix} x & x \\ 0 & 0 \end{pmatrix}\begin{pmatrix} y & y \\ 0 & 0 \end{pmatrix} = \begin{pmatrix} y & y \\ 0 & 0 \end{pmatrix}\begin{pmatrix} x & x \\ 0 & 0 \end{pmatrix}$, so the operation is commutative. Since matrix

multiplication is associative, this operation is associative.

(c)   Since $i \times j = k$ and $j \times i = -k$, the operation is not commutative. Since $(i \times j) \times j = k \times j = -i$ and $i \times (j \times j) = i \times 0 = 0$, the operation is not associative.

(d) $a \circ b = a + b - ab = b + a - ba = b \circ a$ so the operation is commutative.

$$(a \circ b) \circ c = (a + b - ab) \circ c = (a + b - ab) + c - (a + b - ab)c$$
$$= a + b - ab + c - ac - bc + abc$$

and

$$a \circ (b \circ c) = a \circ (b + c - bc) = a + (b + c - bc) - a(b + c - bc)$$
$$= a + b + c - bc - ab - ac + abc.$$

As these expressions are equal, the operation is associative.

Sometimes, if you have two binary operations on a set, such as addition and multiplication for real numbers, you might need to know whether the distributive rule holds. If one operation is denoted by $*$ and the other is denoted by $\circ$, then $*$ is said to be distributive over $\circ$ if $a * (b \circ c) = (a * b) \circ (a * c)$.

> Let $*$ and $\circ$ be two binary operations on a set S. Then $*$ is said to be **distributive** over $\circ$ if $a * (b \circ c) = (a * b) \circ (a * c)$ for all $a, b, c \in S$.

Example 4.1.3

Let $*$ and $\circ$ be defined on $\mathbb{R}$ by $a * b = ab + a + b$ and $a \circ b = a + b + 1$. Investigate whether $*$ is distributive over $\circ$.

Using the definitions,

$$a * (b \circ c) = a * (b + c + 1)$$
$$= a(b + c + 1) + a + (b + c + 1)$$
$$= ab + ac + a + a + b + c + 1$$
$$= ab + ac + 2a + b + c + 1$$

and

$$(a*b)\circ(a*c) = (ab+a+b)\circ(ac+a+c)$$
$$= (ab+a+b)+(ac+a+c)+1$$
$$= ab+a+b+ac+a+c+1$$
$$= ab+ac+2a+b+c+1.$$

As these two expressions are equal, $*$ is distributive over $\circ$.

You can also define binary operations for sets which have only a finite number of elements.

You can use an **operation table** to show the details of a closed binary operation on a small set. Table 4.1 shows the result of 'last digit arithmetic' on $\{2,4,6,8\}$. For example, $2\times 8 = 16$ has last digit 6, so $2\circ 8 = 6$. This is shown in the shaded cell in Table 4.1. Stated formally, the binary operation $\circ$ on the set $\{2,4,6,8\}$ given by $a\circ b$ is the remainder after the product ab is divided by 10.

	$\circ$	Second number 2	4	6	8
	2	4	8	2	6
First	4	8	6	4	2
number	6	2	4	6	8
	8	6	2	8	4

Table 4.1

A binary operation can actually be *defined* by an operation table. For example, Table 4.2 defines a binary operation $\circ$ on the set $\{a,b,c\}$.

$\circ$	a	b	c
a	b	a	c
b	a	c	b
c	b	b	a

Table 4.2

You can see immediately that $\circ$ is a binary operation, and also that it is closed, because Table 4.2 shows the result of every possible combination of two members of the set.

Operation tables are also called **Cayley tables**, after the Englishman Arthur Cayley, 1821–1895. If each element appears exactly once in each row and column, the table is said to be a **Latin square**.

You can also tell quickly from an operation table if a binary operation is commutative by looking for symmetry about the leading diagonal from top left to bottom right. Table 4.2 is not symmetrical since $c\circ a = b$ and $a\circ c = c$ and therefore the operation is not commutative.

Without detailed checking you can't tell from a table whether a binary operation is associative. It is usually easier to exploit some other knowledge you may have about what is described by the table.

Exercise 4A

1 Decide which of the following operations are binary operations on the given sets. If an operation is not a binary operation, give one reason. For those which are binary operations, check whether they are closed, commutative and associative.

(a) $-$ on $\mathbb{Z}^+$

(b) matrix multiplication on 2×2 matrices

(c) $\circ$ on $\mathbb{Z}^+$, where $a\circ b = a^b$

(d) $\circ$ on $\mathbb{R}$, where $a\circ b = |a-b|$

(e) $\circ$ on $\mathbb{R}$, where $a\circ b = 0$ for all $a,b\in\mathbb{R}$

(f) $\circ$ on 2×2 matrices where $A\circ B = AB^{-1}$ for all A and B

(g) $\circ$ on $\mathbb{R}$, where $a\circ b = b$ for all $a,b\in\mathbb{R}$

(h) $\circ$ on $\mathbb{R}^+$, where $a\circ b = a^b$

(i) $\circ$ on $\{1,3,7,9\}$, where $a\circ b$ is the remainder when $a\times b$ is divided by 10

(j) $\circ$ on $\mathbb{R}$, where $a\circ b$ is the smallest number greater than $a+b$

2 Let A, B and C be any three subsets of a universal set U. Use Venn diagrams to investigate whether it is true that

(a) $A\cup(B\cap C)=(A\cup B)\cap(A\cup C)$,   (b) $A\cap(B\cup C)=(A\cap B)\cup(A\cap C)$.

3 Let $\mathbb{Z}_5$ be the set $\{0,1,2,3,4\}$, and define the operations $\otimes$ and $\oplus$ on $\mathbb{Z}_5$ as follows.

$x\otimes y$ is the remainder when xy is divided by 5, $x\oplus y$ is the remainder when $x+y$ is divided by 5.

Investigate whether

(a) $\otimes$ is distributive over $\oplus$,   (b) $\oplus$ is distributive over $\otimes$.

4.2 Identity elements

The numbers 0 and 1 in $\mathbb{R}$ are very special. When the operation is addition, the number 0 has the property that

$$a+0 = 0+a = a$$

for every number a in $\mathbb{R}$.

Similarly, when the operation is multiplication, the number 1 has the property that

$$a\times1 = 1\times a = a$$

for every number a in $\mathbb{R}\setminus\{0\}$.

In each of these examples you have a set S that is closed under a binary operation $\circ$ and an element, often denoted by e, with the property that $a\circ e = e\circ a = a$ for all members of the set S. This element e is called an **identity element** for the set S with the operation $\circ$.

A set with a closed binary operation need not have an identity element.

Example 4.2.1

Show that the set $\mathbb{Z}$ with the operation of subtraction does not have an identity element.

The element 0 is the only element with the property that $a - 0 = a$ for every $a \in \mathbb{Z}$, but as $0 - a = -a$, 0 is not an identity element for $\mathbb{Z}$ under subtraction.

Example 4.2.2

Find the identity element in $\mathbb{R} \setminus \{1\}$ with the binary operation $a \circ b = a + b - ab$.

Let e be an identity element with this binary operation.

$$a \circ e = a \quad \Leftrightarrow \quad a + e - ae = a$$
$$\Leftrightarrow \quad e - ae = 0$$
$$\Leftrightarrow \quad e(1 - a) = 0.$$

For this to be true for all a in $\mathbb{R} \setminus \{1\}$, you need $e = 0$.

As $a \circ b = b \circ a$, there is no need to check separately that $e \circ a = a$.

4.3   Inverse elements

Consider again the two numbers discussed at the beginning of Section 4.2, that is 0 and 1 in $\mathbb{R}$.

For each number $a \in \mathbb{R}$, there exists a number $(-a) \in \mathbb{R}$ such that

$$(-a) + a = a + (-a) = 0.$$

For each number $\mathbb{R} \setminus \{0\}$, there exists a number $a^{-1} \in \mathbb{R} \setminus \{0\}$ such that

$$a^{-1} \times a = a \times a^{-1} = 1.$$

In ordinary algebraic notation these statements look quite different, but $\mathbb{R}$ and $\mathbb{R} \setminus \{0\}$ are both examples of a set S closed under a binary operation $\circ$, with an identity element e. The two statements mean that for each element a in S there exists an element b with the property that $a \circ b = b \circ a = e$. This element b is called an **inverse** of a.

Example 4.3.1

Find an inverse of a in $\mathbb{R} \setminus \{1\}$ with the binary operation $a \circ b = a + b - ab$.

In Example 4.2.2, it was shown that the identity element is 0.

$$b \circ a = e \quad \Leftrightarrow \quad b + a - ba = 0 \quad \Leftrightarrow \quad b = \frac{a}{a - 1}$$

so, as $a \neq 1$, $\dfrac{a}{a - 1}$ is an inverse of a.

As $a \circ b = b \circ a$, there is no need to check separately that $a \circ b = e$.

Example 4.3.2

In Table 4.1, find the identity element and the inverse of 8.

The identity element e is given by $2 \circ e = 2$, $4 \circ e = 4$, $6 \circ e = 6$ and $8 \circ e = 8$. From the table $e = 6$.

The inverse of 8, 8^{-1}, is given by $8^{-1} \circ 8 = e = 6$. From the table, $2 \circ 8 = 6$, so $8^{-1} = 2$.

Summarising the discussion in this and the previous section gives the following:

Let S be a set with a closed binary operation $\circ$.

If there exists an element $e \in S$ such that, for all $a \in S$, $e \circ a = a \circ e = a$, then e is an **identity element** for S with the operation $\circ$.

If for each element $a \in S$ there exists an element $b \in S$ such that $b \circ a = a \circ b = e$, where e is an identity element for S, then b is called an **inverse** of a in S with the operation $\circ$.

Exercise 4B

1 In each of these operation tables, identify the products $s \circ t$, $t \circ s$, $(p \circ q) \circ s$ and $p \circ (q \circ t)$, find the identity element and the inverse of s. Find also the solution for the equations $x \circ t = s$ and $u \circ y = t$.

	p	q	r	s	t	u
p	q	r	p	t	u	s
q	r	p	q	u	s	t
r	p	q	r	s	t	u
s	u	t	s	r	p	q
t	s	u	t	q	r	p
u	t	s	u	p	q	r

	p	u	s	r	q	t
p	r	t	q	p	u	s
u	q	s	r	u	t	p
s	t	r	u	s	p	q
r	p	u	s	r	q	t
q	s	p	t	q	r	u
t	u	q	p	t	s	r

2 In each part of this question a set with a closed binary operation is given. Find the identity element, if it exists, and if it does exist, find the inverse of a general element a, if it exists.

(a) Vectors with 3 components: vector product

(b) 2×2 matrices: matrix multiplication

(c) $\mathbb{C}$: multiplication

(d) $\mathbb{R}$: $\circ$ where $a \circ b = |a - b|$

(e) $\mathbb{R}$: $\circ$ where $a \circ b = b$ for all $a, b \in \mathbb{R}$

3 In each part of this question a set with a closed binary operation is given. Find the identity element, if it exists, and if it does exist, find the inverse of a general element a, if it exists.

(a) The set of matrices of the form $\begin{pmatrix} x & x \\ 0 & 0 \end{pmatrix}$, where $x \in \mathbb{R} \setminus \{0\}$: matrix multiplication

(b) $\{2,4,6,8\}$: $\circ$ where $a \circ b$ is the remainder when $a \times b$ is divided by 10

(c) $\{0,2,4,6,8\}$: $\circ$ where $a \circ b$ is the remainder when $a + b$ is divided by 10

(d) $\{1,3,7,9\}$: $\circ$ where $a \circ b$ is the remainder when $a \times b$ is divided by 10

4.4 Groups

You have seen that sets with binary operations can be distinguished by various properties: the binary operations may or may not be closed or associative, and the sets may or may not have identity and inverse elements. Sets with binary operations which are associative and have identity and inverse elements are especially important.

A set G, with a binary operation $\circ$, is called a **group** if it has four properties, called **axioms**.

1   **Closure**: $a \circ b \in G$ for all $a, b \in G$; that is, the operation is closed.

2   **Associativity**: $a \circ (b \circ c) = (a \circ b) \circ c$ for all $a, b, c \in G$; that is, the binary operation is associative.

3   **Identity**: there exists an identity element $e \in G$ such that for all $a \in G$, $e \circ a = a \circ e = a$.

4   **Inverse**: for each element $a \in G$, there exists an inverse element $b \in G$ such that $b \circ a = a \circ b = e$.

The group G with binary operation $\circ$ is denoted by $(G, \circ)$.

Notice that a group operation need not be commutative.

It is an important fact that there is only one element $e \in G$ with the property that for all $a \in G$, $e \circ a = a \circ e = a$. Once you know that there is only one such element, you can call it *the* identity element for $(G, \circ)$. Similarly, given an element $a \in G$, there is only one inverse element $b \in G$ such that $b \circ a = a \circ b = e$, so you can talk about *the* inverse of a. The notation a^{-1} is used for the inverse of a.

These facts about the uniqueness of the identity and the uniqueness of the inverse for each element are proved at end of the section (see Theorem 4.2). Assume them for now.

Groups may have a finite or an infinite number of elements. Examples of infinite groups are $(\mathbb{Z}, +)$, $(\mathbb{R} \setminus \{0\}, \times)$ and $(\{z \mid z \in \mathbb{C}, |z| = 1\}, \times)$. The set in Example 4.4.1 is an example of a finite group.

The number of elements in a group is called its **order**.

If a group has an infinite number of elements, it is said to have **infinite order**.

To prove that a set with an infinite number of elements is a group, you cannot use arguments based on operation tables.

Example 4.4.1
Prove that the set $\{1, i, -1, -i\}$ with the operation of multiplication is a group.

For a set as small as this, it is often easiest to show that the binary operation is closed by using a table.

Table 4.3 shows the operation table for the set $\{1, i, -1, -i\}$.

×	1	i	−1	−i
1	1	i	−1	−i
i	i	−1	−i	1
−1	−1	−i	1	i
−i	−i	1	i	−1

Table 4.3

To show that the set is a group, there are four properties to establish, namely the four group axioms.

1   **Closure**: The table shows that the operation of multiplication is closed since every possible product is a member of the set $\{1, i, -1, -i\}$.

2   **Associativity**: Multiplication of complex numbers is associative, so multiplication of these elements is associative.

3   **Identity**: The element 1 is the identity element, since $1 \times z = z \times 1 = z$ for every complex number z.

4   **Inverse**: The inverses of 1, −1, i and −i are 1, −1, −i and i respectively, so every element has an inverse which is in the set $\{1, i, -1, -i\}$.

Therefore $\{1, i, -1, -i\}$ with the operation of multiplication is a group.

The row corresponding to the identity element is the same as the row of 'column labels' at the top of the operation table; the column corresponding to the identity element is the same as the column of 'row labels' at the left of the table.

You may have noticed that each element of the group in Table 4.3 appears just once in every row and once in every column, that is, its operation table is a Latin square. This is necessary for a group, as the following theorem shows. However, for a group to have a group table it must be finite.

Theorem 4.1   In the operation table for a finite group, each element appears just once in every row.

In the following argument, a very brief justification is given for each step by referring to one of the group axioms.

Proof
The elements which appear in a row are those of the form $a \circ x$ where a is fixed and x ranges over the elements of the group. Suppose that two elements in a row are the same. Then $a \circ x = a \circ y$ for some x and y, with $x \neq y$. Therefore

$$a \circ x = a \circ y \;\Rightarrow\; a^{-1} \circ (a \circ x) = a^{-1} \circ (a \circ y) \quad \text{(inverse } a^{-1} \text{ exists)}$$
$$\Rightarrow\; \left(a^{-1} \circ a\right) \circ x = \left(a^{-1} \circ a\right) \circ y \quad \text{(associative property)}$$
$$\Rightarrow\; e \circ x = e \circ y \qquad\qquad \text{(property of inverse)}$$
$$\Rightarrow\; x = y. \qquad\qquad\qquad \text{(property of identity)}$$

This is a contradiction, so no element appears more than once in each row.

So, if there are n elements in the group, then there are n elements in the row of the group table, which must all be different. Therefore each element appears just once in each row.

The proof for columns is left to you in Exercise 4C Question 5.

Theorem 4.1 has no meaning for infinite groups, because you can't draw up a table, but the part of the theorem which involves the cancelling argument that

$$a \circ x = a \circ y \;\Rightarrow\; x = y$$

is valid for infinite groups.

Suppose that a and b are known and that you want to solve the equation $a \circ x = b$ for x.

$$a \circ x = b \;\Leftrightarrow\; a^{-1} \circ (a \circ x) = a^{-1} \circ b \quad \text{(inverse } a^{-1} \text{ exists)}$$
$$\Leftrightarrow\; \left(a^{-1} \circ a\right) \circ x = a^{-1} \circ b \quad \text{(associative property)}$$
$$\Leftrightarrow\; e \circ x = a^{-1} \circ b \qquad \text{(property of inverse)}$$
$$\Leftrightarrow\; x = a^{-1} \circ b. \qquad \text{(property of identity)}$$

There are corresponding results if the order of a and x is reversed:

$$x \circ a = y \circ a \;\Rightarrow\; x = y \quad \text{and} \quad x \circ a = b \;\Leftrightarrow\; x = b \circ a^{-1}.$$

In a finite group, each element appears exactly once in each row and each column of the group table.

For any group, $a \circ x = a \circ y \;\Rightarrow\; x = y$ and $x \circ a = y \circ a \;\Rightarrow\; x = y$. This is called the **cancellation law**.

For any group, $a \circ x = b \;\Leftrightarrow\; x = a^{-1} \circ b$ and $x \circ a = b \;\Leftrightarrow\; x = b \circ a^{-1}$.

Although the operation table for a group is always a Latin square, the reverse is not necessarily true. See Exercise 4C Question 2.

Example 4.4.2
Prove that the set of non-singular 2×2 matrices with the operation of matrix multiplication is a group.

The matrices must be non-singular so that inverse matrices exist.

1   **Closure:** The product of two non-singular 2×2 matrices M and N is a 2×2 matrix MN. As M and N are non-singular, $\det M \neq 0$ and $\det N \neq 0$, and since $\det MN = \det M \det N$, $\det MN \neq 0$, so MN is non-singular. So the operation of matrix multiplication is closed.

2   **Associativity**: Since matrix multiplication is associative the group operation is associative.

3   **Identity**: The 2×2 identity matrix I is non-singular and is a member of the set. It has the property that for any matrix M in the set, $IM = MI = M$.

4   **Inverse**: If M is non-singular, then M^{-1} exists and is non-singular, so there exists an element in the set such that $M^{-1}M = MM^{-1} = I$.

Therefore the set of non-singular 2×2 matrices with the operation of matrix multiplication is a group.

There is an important difference between the groups in Examples 4.4.1 and 4.4.2. In Example 4.4.1 the binary operation is commutative, while in Example 4.4.2 it is not.

> In a group $(G, \circ)$, if $a \circ b = b \circ a$ for all $a, b \in G$, the group $(G, \circ)$ is said to be **Abelian** or **commutative**.

The word 'Abelian' is in honour of the Norwegian mathematician Niels Abel (1802–1829).

The next example gives you practice in carrying out calculations in a group. Index notation, which is defined in Section 6.2, is used informally, so that $a^2 = a \circ a$, and so on.

Example 4.4.3
Let $(G, \circ)$ be a group in which $a^3 = e$, $b^2 = e$ and $a \circ b = b \circ a^2$. Show that $b \circ (a^2 \circ b) = a$, $b \circ a = a^2 \circ b$, and simplify the product $(a \circ b)^2$.

Note that, as $a^3 = e$, $a^{-1} = a^2$, and as $b^2 = e$, $b^{-1} = b$.

$$b \circ (a^2 \circ b) = b \circ a \circ (a \circ b) \quad \text{(associative property)}$$
$$= b \circ a \circ (b \circ a^2) \quad \text{(since } a \circ b = b \circ a^2)$$
$$= b \circ (a \circ b) \circ a^2 \quad \text{(associative property)}$$
$$= b \circ (b \circ a^2) \circ a^2 \quad \text{(since } a \circ b = b \circ a^2)$$
$$= b^2 \circ a^4 \quad \text{(associative property)}$$
$$= a. \quad \text{(since } a^3 = e \text{ and } b^2 = e)$$

Since $b \circ (a^2 \circ b) = a$,
$$b \circ a = b \circ (b \circ (a^2 \circ b)) \quad (a = b \circ (a^2 \circ b) \text{ from the first part})$$
$$= b^2 \circ a^2 \circ b \quad \text{(associative property)}$$
$$= e \circ a^2 \circ b \quad \text{(since } b^2 = e)$$
$$= a^2 \circ b. \quad \text{(}e \text{ is the identity)}$$

Notice the strategy: in the first case, the bs were moved steadily across the expression from right to left using the given result $a \circ b = b \circ a^2$ until the results $a^3 = e$, $b^2 = e$ could be used; the second case was simpler, but only because the first part had already been proved.

Now

$$(a \circ b)^2 = (a \circ b) \circ (a \circ b) \qquad \text{(definition of } (a \circ b)^2)$$
$$= a \circ (b \circ a) \circ b \qquad \text{(associative property)}$$
$$= a \circ (a^2 \circ b) \circ b \qquad (b \circ a = a^2 \circ b \text{ from the second part)}$$
$$= a^3 \circ b^2 \qquad \text{(associative property)}$$
$$= e \circ e \qquad \text{(since } a^3 = e \text{ and } b^2 = e)$$
$$= e. \qquad (e \text{ is the identity)}$$

Here are the important algebraic results about groups and inverses promised earlier in this section. These results will be used continually in the chapters which follow.

Theorem 4.2   A group $(G, \circ)$ has the following properties.

(a)   The identity element for a group $(G, \circ)$ is unique.

(b)   For any $a \in G$, the inverse of a is unique.

(c)   For $a, b \in G$, if $a \circ b = e$, then $a = b^{-1}$ and $b = a^{-1}$ and $b \circ a = e$.

(d)   For $a, b \in G$, $(a \circ b)^{-1} = b^{-1} \circ a^{-1}$.

(e)   For $a \in G$, $\left(a^{-1}\right)^{-1} = a$.

One strategy for showing that an element is unique is to suppose that there are two such elements, and then to prove that they must be the same.

Proof

(a)   Suppose that there are two identity elements, e and f.
Since e is an identity, $e \circ a = a$ for any a.
Putting $a = f$ gives $e \circ f = f$.

Since f is an identity, $a \circ f = a$.
Putting $a = e$ gives $e \circ f = e$.

Therefore $f = e$, and the identity element for a group is unique.

(b)   Suppose that a has two inverses, b and c.
Then $a \circ b = b \circ a = e$ and $a \circ c = c \circ a = e$.

So

$$c = c \circ e \qquad (e \text{ is the identity)}$$
$$= c \circ (a \circ b) \qquad \text{(since } a \circ b = e)$$
$$= (c \circ a) \circ b \qquad \text{(associative property)}$$
$$= e \circ b \qquad \text{(since } c \circ a = e)$$
$$= b, \qquad (e \text{ is the identity)}$$

a contradiction, which shows that the inverse of a is unique.

(c)   To prove $a = b^{-1}$, multiply $a \circ b = e$ on the right by b^{-1}. Then

$$a \circ b = e \; \Rightarrow \; (a \circ b) \circ b^{-1} = e \circ b^{-1} \qquad \text{(associative \& identity properties)}$$
$$\Rightarrow \; a \circ \left(b \circ b^{-1}\right) = b^{-1} \qquad \text{(associative property)}$$
$$\Rightarrow \; a \circ e = b^{-1} \qquad \text{(since } b \circ b^{-1} = e\text{)}$$
$$\Rightarrow \; a = b^{-1}. \qquad \text{(}e\text{ is the identity)}$$

The proof of the second part, $b = a^{-1}$, is similar. Then

$$b \circ a = b \circ b^{-1} = e. \qquad \text{(since } a = b^{-1}\text{)}$$

(d)   The proof involves showing that $(a \circ b) \circ \left(b^{-1} \circ a^{-1}\right)$ is e, and using part (c).

$$(a \circ b) \circ \left(b^{-1} \circ a^{-1}\right) = a \circ \left(b \circ \left(b^{-1} \circ a^{-1}\right)\right) \qquad \text{(associative property)}$$
$$= a \circ \left(\left(b \circ b^{-1}\right) \circ a^{-1}\right) \qquad \text{(associative property)}$$
$$= a \circ \left(e \circ a^{-1}\right) \qquad \text{(since } b \circ b^{-1} = e\text{)}$$
$$= a \circ a^{-1} \qquad \text{(}e\text{ is the identity)}$$
$$= e. \qquad \text{(since } a \circ a^{-1} = e\text{)}$$

Then, using part (c) with $a \circ b$ in place of a and $b^{-1} \circ a^{-1}$ in place of b, $(a \circ b)^{-1} = b^{-1} \circ a^{-1}$.

(e)   Since $a \circ a^{-1} = e$, using part (c) with $b = a^{-1}$, $\left(a^{-1}\right)^{-1} = a$.

Exercise 4C

1   Which of the following sets with the given operations are not groups? Give what you believe to be the simplest reason why each is not a group.

(a) $\mathbb{N}$, under addition

(b) $\mathbb{Q}^{+}$, under multiplication

(c) $\{1,2,3,4,5\}: \circ$ where $a \circ b$ is the remainder after ab is divided by 6

(d) $\{1,2,3,4,5,6\}: \circ$ where $a \circ b$ is the remainder after ab is divided by 7

(e) $\{1,2,3,4,5,6\}: \circ$ where $a \circ b$ is the remainder after $a + b$ is divided by 6

(f) $\{0,1,2,3,4,5\}: \circ$ where $a \circ b$ is the remainder after $a + b$ is divided by 6

(g) $\{1,3,5,7,9\}: \circ$ where $a \circ b$ is the remainder after ab is divided by 10

(h)   Rational numbers of the form $\dfrac{m}{2^{n}}$, where $m, n \in \mathbb{Z}$, under addition

(i)   Rational numbers of the form $\dfrac{m}{2^{n}}$, where $m, n \in \mathbb{Z}$, under multiplication

(j)   Numbers of the form 2^{n}, $n \in \mathbb{Z}$, under multiplication

(k)   Matrices of the form $\begin{pmatrix} a & -b \\ b & a \end{pmatrix}$, where $a, b \in \mathbb{R}$, $a^{2} + b^{2} \neq 0$ under matrix multiplication

(l)   Even integers under addition

2 Show that this table is not a group table.

	e	a	b	c
e	e	a	c	b
a	a	c	b	e
b	c	b	e	a
c	b	e	a	c

3 Let the following functions be defined for the domain $x \in \mathbb{R} \setminus \{0,1\}$.

$$i : x \mapsto x \qquad\qquad p : x \mapsto 1-x \qquad\qquad q : x \mapsto \frac{1}{x} \qquad\qquad r : x \mapsto \frac{1}{1-x}$$

Show that these functions, together with two more functions which you should find, form a group under composition of functions.

4 Prove that in a finite group table, each element appears just once in every column.

5 Prove that $(\mathbb{Z} \setminus \{0\}, \times)$ is not a group.

6 A group G has four elements. Three of these are e (the identity), a and b. Give reasons why the element $a \circ b$ cannot be equal to e, to a or to b.

7 Prove that the set of nth roots of unity forms a group under multiplication.

8 Show that functions of the form $f(x) = ax + b$, where $a, b \in \mathbb{R}$ and $a \neq 0$, form a group under the operation of composition of functions. What is the inverse of $x \mapsto ax + b$?

9 Let $(G, \circ)$ be a group in which $a^4 = e$, $b^2 = e$ and $a \circ b = b \circ a^3$.
Show that $b \circ a = a^3 \circ b$, $b \circ (a^2 \circ b) = a^2$, and simplify the product $(a \circ b) \circ (a^2 \circ b)$.

10 Consider the set $(\mathbb{R} \times \mathbb{R}) \setminus \{0,0\}$ with the binary operation $\circ$ defined by

$$(a,b) \circ (c,d) = (ad + bc, bd - ac).$$

Show that this set with this operation is a group.

11 Let $(G, \circ)$ and $(H, *)$ be groups, and consider the set $G \times H$ with the binary operation $\times$ defined by $(g_1, h_1) \times (g_2, h_2) = (g_1 \circ g_2, h_1 * h_2)$. Show that $G \times H$ with this operation is a group.

5 Some examples of groups

This chapter introduces you to a variety of groups. When you have completed it, you should

- know that the integers modulo n under addition form a group
- know the groups of symmetries of an equilateral triangle, rectangle and square
- know that permutations form a group.

5.1 Modular arithmetic and addition

Modular arithmetic is a kind of 'arithmetic with remainders'. When you divide a natural number by n, the remainder is one of the numbers $0, 1, 2, \dots, n-1$. So consider the set $\mathbb{Z}_n = \{0,1,2,\dots,n-1\}$ with the following rule for combining the elements:

$a \oplus b$ is the remainder when $a+b$ is divided by n.

To show that $\mathbb{Z}_n$ with this rule is a group, use the axioms in Section 4.4.

1   **Closure:** As the remainder after division by n belongs to $\mathbb{Z}_n$, the operation is closed.

2   **Associativity:** Suppose that $a+b = nr + x$, where $x \in \mathbb{Z}_n$, and $x+c = ns+y$, where $y \in \mathbb{Z}_n$.

Then $x = a \oplus b$, and $y = x \oplus c = (a \oplus b) \oplus c$.

Now
$$
\begin{aligned}
(a+b)+c &= (nr + x) + c \\
&= nr + (x+c) \\
&= nr + (ns + y) \\
&= (nr + ns) + y \\
&= n(r+s) + y,
\end{aligned}
$$

so $y = (a \oplus b) \oplus c$ is the remainder when $(a+b)+c$ is divided by n.

Similarly, $a \oplus (b \oplus c)$ is the remainder when $a + (b+c)$ is divided by n.

But $(a+b)+c = a+(b+c)$, so $(a \oplus b) \oplus c = a \oplus (b \oplus c)$.

3   **Identity:** The number 0 acts as the identity since $a \oplus 0 = 0 \oplus a = a$ for all $a \in \mathbb{Z}_n$.

4   **Inverse:** If $a = 0$, consider 0. Then $0 \oplus 0 = 0$, so 0 is the inverse of 0.

Now consider $a \neq 0$, where $a \in \mathbb{Z}_n$. Consider $n-a$.

As $n > n - a > 0$, $n - a \in \mathbb{Z}_n$; and $(n-a) \oplus a = ((n-a)+a) - n = 0$ and $a \oplus (n-a) = (a + (n-a)) - n = 0$.

Therefore $n-a$ is the inverse of a.

Therefore $\mathbb{Z}_n$ with this rule is a group.

The group is called $(\mathbb{Z}_n, \oplus)$, the group of **integers modulo n (mod n) under addition**, and the operation is sometimes written as $+(\bmod n)$.

Notice that, now that the basic properties of modular arithmetic have been established, there is no need to go on using the 'ringed' addition sign. You can use the ordinary addition sign without ambiguity, and write $(\mathbb{Z}_n, +)$.

The word 'modulo' is used in a totally different way from the word 'modulus'.

Example 5.1.1
Find the remainder when the numbers 23 and –23 are written in modulo 4 .

$23 = 5 \times 4 + 3$, so the remainder is 3.

$-23 = (-6) \times 4 + 1$, so the remainder is 1.

Example 5.1.2
(a) Write out the group table for $(\mathbb{Z}_4, +)$.   (b) Solve the equations $x + 1 = 0$ and $2 + y = 1$.

(a)

+	0	1	2	3
0	0	1	2	3
1	1	2	3	0
2	2	3	0	1
3	3	0	1	2

Table 5.1

(b)   From Table 5.1, the inverse of 1 is 3, so

$$(x + 1) + 3 = 0 + 3$$
$$x + (1 + 3) = 0 + 3$$
$$x + 0 = 3$$
$$x = 3.$$

The inverse of 2 is 2, so

$$2 + (2 + y) = 2 + 1$$
$$(2 + 2) + y = 3$$
$$0 + y = 3$$
$$y = 3.$$

5.2* Modular arithmetic and multiplication

If you wish you can omit the theory of this section. However in order to do some of the exercises, you will need to know that $(\mathbb{Z}_p \setminus \{0\}, \times)$, where p is prime, is a group.

As well as doing modular arithmetic with addition, you can also do it with multiplication, using the definition

$a \otimes b$ is the remainder when ab is divided by n.

However, there are two important differences between multiplication and addition.

- The number 0 has the property that $0 \times a = a \times 0 = 0$ for all $a \in \mathbb{Z}_n$. It follows that $(\mathbb{Z}_n, \otimes)$ cannot be a group, since 0 does not have an inverse. So it is best to consider $\mathbb{Z}_n \setminus \{0\}$, that is the set $\{1, 2, \ldots, n-1\}$.

- If n is not prime, then $(\mathbb{Z} \setminus \{0\}, \otimes)$ is not closed. For example, in $\mathbb{Z}_6$, $2 \otimes 3 = 0$ which is not in $\mathbb{Z}_6 \setminus \{0\}$. So you can only get a group if n is a prime number.

So consider the set $\mathbb{Z}_p \setminus \{0\} = \{1, 2, \ldots, p-1\}$, where p is a prime number.

1   **Closure**: Since the remainder after division by p belongs to $\mathbb{Z}_n \setminus \{0\}$, the operation is closed.

Note that the remainder cannot be 0 because that would mean that $ab = xp$ and as the right side is divisible by p, the left side is also divisible by p. But $0 < a, b \le p-1$ so this is impossible.

2   **Associativity**: Let $ab = pr + x$, where $x \in \mathbb{Z}_p \setminus \{0\}$, and $xc = ps + y$ where $y \in \mathbb{Z}_p \setminus \{0\}$.

Then $x = a \otimes b$, and $y = x \otimes c = (a \otimes b) \otimes c$.

Now
$$
\begin{aligned}
(ab)c &= (pr + x)c \\
&= (pr)c + (xc) \\
&= p(rc) + (ps + y) \\
&= (p(rc) + ps) + y \\
&= p(rc + s) + y,
\end{aligned}
$$

so $y = (a \otimes b) \otimes c$ is the remainder when $(ab)c$ is divided by p.

Similarly, $a \otimes (b \otimes c)$ is the remainder when $a(bc)$ is divided by p.

But $(ab)c = a(bc)$, so $(a \otimes b) \otimes c = a \otimes (b \otimes c)$.

3   **Identity**: The number 1 acts as the identity since $a \otimes 1 = 1 \otimes a = a$ for all $a \in \mathbb{Z}_p \setminus \{0\}$.

4   **Inverse**: For $a \in \mathbb{Z}_p \setminus \{0\}$, consider the elements $\{1 \otimes a, 2 \otimes a, \ldots, (p-1) \otimes a\}$.

These elements are all different, since if two of them, say $r \otimes a$ and $s \otimes a$, are equal, then $r \otimes a$ and $s \otimes a$ have the same remainder on division by p.

Suppose that $ra = kp + x$ and $sa = lp + x$ where k and l are integers and $x \in \mathbb{Z}_p \setminus \{0\}$. Then

$$ra - kp = sa - lp,$$

so $$ra - sa = kp - lp,$$

that is,

$$(r - s)a = (k - l)p.$$

Now p divides the right side; so p divides the left side, and must divide either a or $r - s$.

But $a \in \mathbb{Z}_p \setminus \{0\}$, so p does not divide a; and $-(p-1) \le r - s \le p-1$, so the only possibility is that $r - s = 0$, or $r = s$.

So no two members of the set $\{1 \otimes a, 2 \otimes a, \ldots, (p-1) \otimes a\}$ are equal.

As they are all different, and there are $p - 1$ of them, one of them must be 1.

Suppose that $b \otimes a = 1$.

Then $a \otimes b = 1$, from the definition of $\otimes$, so b is the inverse of a.

The proof that the inverse exists is interesting because it does not actually produce the inverse of each element. It only shows that each element must have an inverse.

So $\mathbb{Z}_p \setminus \{0\}$ with this rule is a group which is called $(\mathbb{Z}_n \setminus \{0\}, \otimes)$, the group of **non-zero integers modulo p (mod p) under multiplication**. In order to distinguish this operation from ordinary multiplication, it is sometimes written as $\times (\operatorname{mod} n)$.

Notice that, as for addition, the multiplication sign rather than the 'ringed' multiplication sign is used. Table 5.2 shows $(\mathbb{Z}_5 \setminus \{0\}, \times)$.

$\times$	1	2	3	4
1	1	2	3	4
2	2	4	1	3
3	3	1	4	2
4	4	3	2	1

Table 5.2

From Table 5.2, the inverse of 3 is 2, and vice versa. But if you had to find, say, the inverse of 7 in $(\mathbb{Z}_{59} \setminus \{0\}, \times)$, it would not be so easy.

Example 5.2.1
Find the inverse of 5 in $(\mathbb{Z}_{11} \setminus \{0\}, \times)$.

$$2 \times 5 = 10,\ 3 \times 5 = 4,\ 4 \times 5 = 9,\ 5 \times 5 = 3,\ 6 \times 5 = 8,\ 7 \times 5 = 2,\ 8 \times 5 = 7,\ 9 \times 5 = 1.$$

Since $5^{-1} \times 5 = 1$ and $9 \times 5 = 1$, the inverse of 5 is 9.

You can often use 'brute force' in this way to find inverses in a small group.

Note that in Example 5.2.1, if you want inverses of other elements, things get progressively easier. You now know that the inverse of 5 is 9, so the inverse of 9 is 5. To find 3^{-1} use $5 \times 5 = 3$ to give

$$3^{-1} = (5 \times 5)^{-1} = 5^{-1} \times 5^{-1} = 9 \times 9 = 4,$$

so $3^{-1} = 4$. And this also shows that $4^{-1} = 3$.

If you want 2^{-1}, you need now try only 2, 6, 7, 8 and 10. Once you spot $2^{-1} = 6$, you can deduce from $6 \times 5 = 8$ that

$$8^{-1} = (6 \times 5)^{-1} = 5^{-1} \times 6^{-1} = 9 \times 2 = 7.$$

This leaves 10 as its own inverse.

Example 5.2.2

Construct an operation table for the numbers 1, 5, 7, 11, 13, 17 when combined under the operation $\times(\text{mod}\,18)$. Show that these numbers with this operation form a group, and write down the inverse of each element. Solve the equation $13x = 11$.

The operation table is shown in Table 5.3.

$\times(\text{mod}\,18)$	1	5	7	11	13	17
1	1	5	7	11	13	17
5	5	7	17	1	11	13
7	7	17	13	5	1	11
11	11	1	5	13	17	7
13	13	11	1	17	7	5
17	17	13	11	7	5	1

Table 5.3

The numbers form a group, because

- the table shows that the operation is a closed binary operation
- the operation is associative, because ordinary multiplication is associative
- the identity is 1
- each element has an inverse; the inverses of 1, 5, 7, 11, 13 and 17 are respectively, 1, 11, 13, 5, 7 and 17.

As the inverse of 13 is 7, multiplying $13x = 11$ by 7 gives $x = 7 \times 11 = 5$.

It is true, but won't be proved here, that the positive integers which are less than n and have no factors in common with n form a group under the operation $\times(\text{mod}\,n)$.

Exercise 5A

1   Write out the group table for $(\mathbb{Z}_5, +)$, and write down the inverse of 2. Solve the equations $x + 2 = 1$ and $4 + y = 2$.

2   Write out a group table for $(\mathbb{Z}_7 \setminus \{0\}, \times)$. Write down the inverses of 3 and 4.

3   Write out a table of operations for $(\mathbb{Z}_6 \setminus \{0\}, \times)$. Give one reason why $(\mathbb{Z}_6 \setminus \{0\}, \times)$ is not a group. Give a reason why $(\mathbb{Z}_q \setminus \{0\}, \times)$ is not a group if q is not prime.

4   Construct a combination table for the integers $\{1,2,4,7,8,11,13,14\}$ under the operation $\times(\text{mod}\,15)$. Use your table to solve the equation $13x = 8\,(\text{mod}\,15)$.

5   Solve the equation $13x = 17$ using the operation $\times(\text{mod}\,20)$.

6   Calculate 7×9 and 4×15 in $(\mathbb{Z}_{59} \setminus \{0\}, \times)$. Use your answers to find the inverses of
   (a) 4,   (b) 7,   (c) 28,   (d) 49.

7 Construct a combination table for the numbers $\{0,1,2,3,4\}$ under the operation $\oplus$ where $a \oplus b = (a + b + 2)(\text{mod } 5)$, and verify that it is a group table. Write down the identity element and the inverse of each element.

5.3 A group of symmetries

Let **E** be the equilateral triangle ABC shown in Fig. 5.4, and let the lines x, y and z and the points 1, 2 and 3 be fixed in the plane. Define the following transformations of the plane containing **E**.

- X is 'reflect in the line x'.
- Y is 'reflect in the line y'.
- Z is 'reflect in the line z'.
- R is 'rotate by $\frac{2}{3}\pi$ anticlockwise about O'.
- S is 'rotate by $\frac{4}{3}\pi$ anticlockwise about O'.
- I is 'do nothing'.

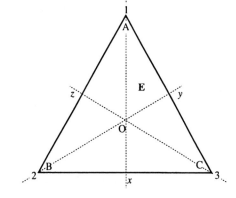

Each of these transformations of the plane leaves the triangle where it is now, although it may change the positions of the vertices which make up the triangle **E**. This kind of transformation is called a **symmetry** of **E**.

Fig. 5.4

You can describe the transformation X by writing

$$\begin{pmatrix} 1 & 2 & 3 \\ A & B & C \end{pmatrix} \xrightarrow{\ X\ } \begin{pmatrix} 1 & 2 & 3 \\ A & C & B \end{pmatrix}$$

where the notation in the first bracket shows that A started in position 1, B in position 2 and C in position 3, and after the transformation by X, A is still in position 1, B is now in position 3 and C is in position 2.

To combine operations use the rule 'followed by', that is the usual rule for combining functions.

The transformation RX (X followed by R) is

$$\begin{pmatrix} 1 & 2 & 3 \\ A & B & C \end{pmatrix} \xrightarrow{\ X\ } \begin{pmatrix} 1 & 2 & 3 \\ A & C & B \end{pmatrix} \xrightarrow{\ R\ } \begin{pmatrix} 1 & 2 & 3 \\ B & A & C \end{pmatrix}$$

which is the same as transformation Z. Thus $RX = Z$. Similarly $SR = I$.

You can make up Table 5.5, which shows how each of the transformations I, R, S, X, Y and Z combines with the others, using the rule 'followed by'. The result is always one of I, R, S, X, Y and Z, so 'followed by' is a closed binary operation on the set $\{I, R, S, X, Y, Z\}$.

In Table 5.5, the result $RX = Z$ is shown by going along the row containing R and down the column containing X.

		First operation performed					
		I	R	S	X	Y	Z
	I	I	R	S	X	Y	Z
Second	R	R	S	I	Z	X	Y
operation	S	S	I	R	Y	Z	X
performed	X	X	Y	Z	I	R	S
	Y	Y	Z	X	S	I	R
	Z	Z	X	Y	R	S	I

Table 5.5

As 'followed by' is the rule of combination of functions, it is associative.

The transformation I is the identity element.

Each element has an inverse. The inverses of I, R, S, X, Y and Z are I, S, R, X, Y and Z respectively.

So the set $\{I, R, S, X, Y, Z\}$ together with the operation 'followed by' is a group. It is called the **dihedral group of the triangle** and is given the symbol D_3. Similar groups are defined for all regular polygons: the symbol for the dihedral group of the n-sided polygon is D_n.

The word 'dihedral' means having or being contained by two plane faces.

Exercise 5B

1 Write out the group table for the symmetries of a non-square rectangle. Use X and Y for reflections in the x- and y-axes respectively, and H for half-turn.

2 In the group D_3 in Table 5.5 find the elements R^{-1} and X^{-1}. Calculate the products RAR^{-1} and XAX^{-1} when $A = I, R, S, X, Y$ and Z in turn. Solve for A the equation $RAX = Y$.

3 Write out the group table for D_4, the dihedral group of the square. (Keep this group table for use with Question 4 and future exercises.)
(Take the origin to be at the centre of the square and let R be an anticlockwise quarter-turn about the origin, and use the notation R^2 and R^3 for the other rotations. Let H and V be reflections in the x- and y-axes, and L and M be reflections in the lines $y = -x$ and $y = x$. Put the operations in the order, I, R, R^2, R^3, H, L, V, M. Your table should then match the one given in the answers.)

4 In D_4 solve for A the equation $RAV = H$. (Use your table from Question 3.)

5.4 Permutations

Suppose that you have a set of four distinct objects. A permutation of these objects is a rearrangement of them among themselves. Thus if the objects are red, white, blue and green counters, then you could permute them by replacing the green counter by the blue one, and vice versa. Or you could replace blue by green, red by blue, and green by red. Both of these are examples of permutations. In practice, it is more convenient to label the four objects 1, 2, 3 and 4. Then the permutation which interchanges blue and green would be 'replace 1, 2, 3, 4 by 1, 2, 4, 3'. This permutation is called

$$\begin{pmatrix} 1 & 2 & 3 & 4 \\ 1 & 2 & 4 & 3 \end{pmatrix}$$

where each number is replaced by the number underneath it, to show that 4 replaces 3 and 3 replaces 4.

Similarly the permutation which replaces 1, 2, 3, 4 by 3, 2, 4, 1 is called

$$\begin{pmatrix} 1 & 2 & 3 & 4 \\ 3 & 2 & 4 & 1 \end{pmatrix}$$

showing that 3 replaces 1, 4 replaces 3 and 1 replaces 4.

Notice that the original order 1, 2, 3, 4 is not important. The permutation $\begin{pmatrix} 4 & 2 & 1 & 3 \\ 3 & 2 & 1 & 4 \end{pmatrix}$ means the same

as $\begin{pmatrix} 1 & 2 & 3 & 4 \\ 1 & 2 & 4 & 3 \end{pmatrix}$; both of them show that 4 replaces 3 and 3 replaces 4. Similarly, $\begin{pmatrix} 1 & 2 & 3 & 4 \\ 3 & 2 & 4 & 1 \end{pmatrix}$,

$\begin{pmatrix} 4 & 2 & 1 & 3 \\ 1 & 2 & 3 & 4 \end{pmatrix}, \begin{pmatrix} 2 & 3 & 4 & 1 \\ 2 & 4 & 1 & 3 \end{pmatrix}$ and $\begin{pmatrix} 2 & 1 & 4 & 3 \\ 2 & 3 & 1 & 4 \end{pmatrix}$ are identical permutations.

If the permutation $\begin{pmatrix} 1 & 2 & 3 & 4 \\ 1 & 2 & 4 & 3 \end{pmatrix}$ is followed by $\begin{pmatrix} 1 & 2 & 3 & 4 \\ 3 & 2 & 4 & 1 \end{pmatrix}$, then the effect is the permutation $\begin{pmatrix} 1 & 2 & 3 & 4 \\ 3 & 2 & 1 & 4 \end{pmatrix}$. It can be useful to consider the two permutations in the product 'above' one another, in the form

$$\begin{pmatrix} 1 & 2 & 3 & 4 \\ 1 & 2 & 4 & 3 \\ 3 & 2 & 1 & 4 \end{pmatrix}.$$

The first two rows show the effect of the first permutation, while the second two rows show the effect of the second permutation. The result of the first permutation followed by the second permutation is the permutation formed by taking the first and last rows, namely $\begin{pmatrix} 1 & 2 & 3 & 4 \\ 3 & 2 & 1 & 4 \end{pmatrix}$, showing that 3 replaces 1, and 1 replaces 3.

5.5 Another look at permutations

You can think of the ideas in Section 5.4 in a different way. Let A be the set $\{1,2,3,4\}$. Then the permutation $\begin{pmatrix} 1 & 2 & 3 & 4 \\ 1 & 2 & 4 & 3 \end{pmatrix}$ is really a bijection of the set A to itself, defined in Fig. 5.6.

In the same way, Fig. 5.7 shows the effect of the permutation $\begin{pmatrix} 1 & 2 & 3 & 4 \\ 3 & 2 & 4 & 1 \end{pmatrix}$.

This leads to the following definition.

A **permutation** of a set A is a bijection from A to A.

1	→	1
2	→	2
3	→	2
4	→	4

1	→	3
2	→	2
3	→	4
4	→	1

Fig. 5.6   Fig. 5.7

Looking at it this way, you can see that the composition of permutations described in Section 5.4 is nothing more than the composition of functions from Section 3.6.

For example, returning to the case when $A = \{1,2,3,4\}$, for the permutation $\begin{pmatrix} 1 & 2 & 3 & 4 \\ 1 & 2 & 4 & 3 \end{pmatrix}$ followed by $\begin{pmatrix} 1 & 2 & 3 & 4 \\ 3 & 2 & 4 & 1 \end{pmatrix}$, you could draw the diagram in Fig. 5.8.

$$
\begin{array}{ccccc}
1 & \to & 1 & \to & 3 \\
2 & \to & 2 & \to & 2 \\
3 & \to & 4 & \to & 1 \\
4 & \to & 3 & \to & 4
\end{array}
$$

Fig. 5.8

This leads, as before, to the permutation $\begin{pmatrix} 1 & 2 & 3 & 4 \\ 3 & 2 & 1 & 4 \end{pmatrix}$.

You may think that it is easier to think of a permutation as a function, and to use the notation of Fig. 5.8 instead of the bracket notation. You may be right, but the bracket notation is traditional, and a little reflection should convince you that they are equivalent. Moreover, the bracket notation saves space.

It follows immediately the work on functions in Chapter 3 that the set S_A of permutations of a set A under the operation of composition of functions is a group.

In the particular case when A is the finite set $\{1, 2, \ldots, n\}$, the group of all permutations of A is called the **symmetric group of degree n**, and is written S_n.

Example 5.5.1

Calculate the result of the permutation $\begin{pmatrix} 1 & 2 & 3 \\ 2 & 3 & 1 \end{pmatrix}$ on three elements followed by the permutation $\begin{pmatrix} 1 & 2 & 3 \\ 3 & 1 & 2 \end{pmatrix}$.

To do this you need to 'chase' each element through both permutations.

In the first permutation $1 \to 2$, and in the second, $2 \to 1$, so composing the two permutations gives $1 \to 1$. Similarly, $2 \to 3 \to 2$, and $3 \to 1 \to 3$. So the combined permutation is $\begin{pmatrix} 1 & 2 & 3 \\ 1 & 2 & 3 \end{pmatrix}$.

This is the identity permutation, in which each element is mapped to itself. Notice also that the permutations $\begin{pmatrix} 1 & 2 & 3 \\ 2 & 3 & 1 \end{pmatrix}$ and $\begin{pmatrix} 1 & 2 & 3 \\ 3 & 1 & 2 \end{pmatrix}$ are inverse.

The word 'inverse' is used in two senses here, and these two senses coincide. The two permutations, which are bijections, are inverse bijections. And each of them is also the inverse element of the other in the group sense of the word inverse.

Example 5.5.2

Let $x = \begin{pmatrix} 1 & 2 & 3 & 4 & 5 \\ 3 & 1 & 5 & 4 & 2 \end{pmatrix}$ and $y = \begin{pmatrix} 1 & 2 & 3 & 4 & 5 \\ 2 & 3 & 4 & 5 & 1 \end{pmatrix}$. Calculate xy and yx.

Notice how the use of product notation has been slipped into permutations. As usual xy means permutation y followed by permutation x. This notation is consistent with the notation for functions $f(g(a)) = (fg)(a)$.

Chasing through the elements again, for the permutation xy, $1 \to 2 \to 1$, $2 \to 3 \to 5$, $3 \to 4 \to 4$, $4 \to 5 \to 2$, and $5 \to 1 \to 3$. The permutation xy is given by

$$xy = \begin{pmatrix} 1 & 2 & 3 & 4 & 5 \\ 1 & 5 & 4 & 2 & 3 \end{pmatrix}.$$

Similarly, the permutation yx is given by

$$yx = \begin{pmatrix} 1 & 2 & 3 & 4 & 5 \\ 4 & 2 & 1 & 5 & 3 \end{pmatrix}.$$

Notice that for permutations, just as for all functions, xy is not generally equal to yx.

Composition of permutations of three or more elements is not commutative.

Example 5.5.3

Let $x = \begin{pmatrix} 1 & 2 & 3 & 4 & 5 \\ 3 & 1 & 5 & 4 & 2 \end{pmatrix}$. Find the permutation x^{-1}.

You could do this in one of two ways. You might notice that $x^{-1} = \begin{pmatrix} 3 & 1 & 5 & 4 & 2 \\ 1 & 2 & 3 & 4 & 5 \end{pmatrix}$ and then rearrange the elements in the top row so that they come in the conventional order, at the same time moving the bottom row in a corresponding way.

Thus $x^{-1} = \begin{pmatrix} 1 & 2 & 3 & 4 & 5 \\ 2 & 5 & 1 & 4 & 3 \end{pmatrix}$.

On the other hand, you could chase elements.

Starting with 1, since x takes $1 \to 3$, x^{-1} takes $3 \to 1$. So x^{-1} starts $x^{-1} = \begin{pmatrix} & & 3 & & \\ & & 1 & & \end{pmatrix}$. Then

x takes $2 \to 1$, so x^{-1} takes $1 \to 2$. So x^{-1} continues with $x^{-1} = \begin{pmatrix} 1 & & 3 & & \\ 2 & & 1 & & \end{pmatrix}$.

And so on until $x^{-1} = \begin{pmatrix} 1 & 2 & 3 & 4 & 5 \\ 2 & 5 & 1 & 4 & 3 \end{pmatrix}$.

Example 5.5.4

Write out a Cayley table (or group table) for the composition of permutations in S_3.

The possible permutations in S_3 are given by the six possible ways of ordering the numbers a, b and c as 1, 2 and 3 in the second row of the permutation $\begin{pmatrix} 1 & 2 & 3 \\ a & b & c \end{pmatrix}$.

They are therefore the six permutations below.

$$e = \begin{pmatrix} 1 & 2 & 3 \\ 1 & 2 & 3 \end{pmatrix} \quad r = \begin{pmatrix} 1 & 2 & 3 \\ 2 & 3 & 1 \end{pmatrix} \quad s = \begin{pmatrix} 1 & 2 & 3 \\ 3 & 1 & 2 \end{pmatrix}$$

$$x = \begin{pmatrix} 1 & 2 & 3 \\ 1 & 3 & 2 \end{pmatrix} \quad y = \begin{pmatrix} 1 & 2 & 3 \\ 3 & 2 & 1 \end{pmatrix} \quad z = \begin{pmatrix} 1 & 2 & 3 \\ 2 & 1 & 3 \end{pmatrix}$$

The group table for S_3 is shown in Table 5.9.

S_3	e	r	s	x	y	z
e	e	r	s	x	y	z
r	r	s	e	z	x	y
s	s	e	r	y	z	x
x	x	y	z	e	r	s
y	y	z	x	s	e	r
z	z	x	y	r	s	e

Table 5.9

Exercise 5C

1 The permutations a, b and c are taken from S_5.

$$a = \begin{pmatrix} 1 & 2 & 3 & 4 & 5 \\ 5 & 3 & 4 & 1 & 2 \end{pmatrix} \quad b = \begin{pmatrix} 1 & 2 & 3 & 4 & 5 \\ 2 & 3 & 4 & 5 & 1 \end{pmatrix} \quad c = \begin{pmatrix} 1 & 2 & 3 & 4 & 5 \\ 5 & 3 & 2 & 4 & 1 \end{pmatrix}$$

Calculate the permutations: ab, ba, a^2b, ac^{-1}, $(ac)^{-1}$, $c^{-1}ac$.

2 Using the permutations from Question 1, solve for x the equations $ax = b$ and $axb = c$.

3 In S_3, let $a = \begin{pmatrix} 1 & 2 & 3 \\ 2 & 3 & 1 \end{pmatrix}$ and $b = \begin{pmatrix} 1 & 2 & 3 \\ 3 & 2 & 1 \end{pmatrix}$.

Calculate the following permutations.

(a) ab

(b) ba

(c) a^{-1}

(d) b^{-1}

(e) aba^{-1}

(f) bab^{-1}

(g) ab^2a^{-1}

(h) ba^2b^{-1}

6 Subgroups

This chapter extends the study of groups by investigating groups within other groups. When you have completed it, you should know

- what is meant by the order of an element
- what is meant by a cyclic group, and how to show that a group is, or is not, cyclic
- what a subgroup is, and how to test for a subgroup
- that the order of a subgroup divides the order of the group
- that the order of an element divides the order of the group
- that all groups of prime order are cyclic.

6.1 Notation

It can be tedious to use the notation $(G, \circ)$ for a group, and it is quite usual to leave out the symbol for the operation and to use multiplicative notation. From now on, provided there is no ambiguity, the symbol G will be used for a group and ab will be used instead of $a \circ b$.

However, in some groups, such as $\mathbb{Z}$, the operation is addition, and then it is usual to retain the $+$ sign. It is a convention that, whenever additive notation is used, the group is commutative. If multiplicative notation is used, the group may be either commutative or not commutative.

Here is an example of a proof in the new notation.

Example 6.1.1

Let G be a group in which every element is its own inverse. Prove that G is commutative.

Let $a, b \in G$. Then $ab \in G$. As $ab \in G$, it is its own inverse, so $(ab)^{-1} = ab$. But the inverse of ab is $b^{-1}a^{-1}$ so $b^{-1}a^{-1} = ab$, and as $a^{-1} = a$ and $b^{-1} = b$, $ba = ab$. So G is commutative.

6.2 Powers of elements

In Example 4.4.3, you saw that when you multiply an element a of a group G by itself, you obtain aa, which is written as a^2. This leads to the following definition.

Let a be an element of a group G. If n is a positive integer, then

$$a^n = \overbrace{aa\ldots a}^{n \text{ times}} \quad \text{and} \quad a^{-n} = \overbrace{a^{-1}a^{-1}\ldots a^{-1}}^{n \text{ times}}.$$

The power a^0 is defined to be e.

Many of the usual index rules are satisfied for all integers $m, n \in \mathbb{Z}$, but they require proof. Here are two examples of such proofs. If you wish, you may omit them and assume the results of the next shaded box.

Example 6.2.1*

Show that $a^m a^n = a^{m+n}$ when m is a positive integer and n is a negative integer.

Let $n = -N$, so that N is positive. Then $a^m a^{-N} = \overbrace{aa \ldots aa}^{m \text{ times}} \overbrace{{}^{-1} a^{-1} \ldots a^{-1}}^{N \text{ times}}$.

Case 1   Suppose that $m > N$. Then

$$a^m a^{-N} = \overbrace{aa \ldots aa}^{m \text{ times}} \overbrace{{}^{-1} a^{-1} \ldots a^{-1}}^{N \text{ times}} = \overbrace{aa \ldots a}^{(m-N) \text{ times}} = \overbrace{aa \ldots a}^{(m+n) \text{ times}} = a^{m+n}.$$

Case 2   Suppose that $m = N$. Then

$$a^m a^{-N} = \overbrace{aa \ldots aa}^{m \text{ times}} \overbrace{{}^{-1} a^{-1} \ldots a^{-1}}^{m \text{ times}} = e = a^0 = a^{m-N} = a^{m+n}.$$

Case 3   Suppose that $m < N$. Then

$$a^m a^{-N} = \overbrace{aa \ldots aa}^{m \text{ times}} \overbrace{{}^{-1} a^{-1} \ldots a^{-1}}^{N \text{ times}} = \overbrace{a^{-1} a^{-1} \ldots a^{-1}}^{(N-m) \text{ times}} = a^{-(N-m)} = a^{m-N} = a^{m+n}.$$

Therefore, in all cases, $a^m a^n = a^{m+n}$ when m is a positive integer and n is a negative integer.

Example 6.2.2*

Show that $a^{-m} = \left(a^m\right)^{-1} = \left(a^{-1}\right)^m$ when m is a positive integer.

From Case 2 above, $a^m a^{-m} = e$, so a^{-m} is the inverse of a^m, that is $a^{-m} = \left(a^m\right)^{-1}$.

By definition, $\overbrace{a^{-1} a^{-1} \ldots a^{-1}}^{m \text{ times}} = a^{-m}$; but $\overbrace{a^{-1} a^{-1} \ldots a^{-1}}^{m \text{ times}} = \left(a^{-1}\right)^m$. So $a^{-m} = \left(a^{-1}\right)^m$.

Therefore $a^{-m} = \left(a^m\right)^{-1} = \left(a^{-1}\right)^m$ when m is a positive integer.

The results of the above examples, and others like them, are summarised by:

In a group G, $a^m a^n = a^{m+n}$, $\left(a^m\right)^n = a^{mn}$, $a^{-m} = \left(a^m\right)^{-1} = \left(a^{-1}\right)^m$, where m and $n \in \mathbb{Z}$.

In general $(ab)^m \neq a^m b^m$, unless the group G is commutative.

It is clear that in a finite group the powers of an element cannot all be different from each other.

For example, in $\left(\mathbb{Z}_7 \setminus \{0\}, \times\right)$,

$$2^2 = 4, \quad 2^3 = 2 \times 4 = 1, \quad 2^4 = 2 \times 1 = 2, \quad 2^5 = 2 \times 2^4 = 2 \times 2 = 4, \quad 2^6 = 2^2 \times 2^4 = 4 \times 2 = 1,$$

and so on.

In D_3 (from Section 5.3) which is reproduced as Table 6.1 in Example 6.2.3,

$$R^2 = S, \quad R^3 = RS = I, \quad R^4 = RI = R, \quad R^5 = RR = S, \quad \text{and so on.}$$

Theorem 6.1   Let a be an element of a finite group G. Then the powers of a cannot all be different, and there is a smallest positive integer k such that $a^k = e$.

Proof

Consider the set of all possible powers of a.

There are infinitely many of them, and all of them are elements of G.

Since G is finite they cannot all be different.

Let r and s be two positive integers, with $r < s$, such that $a^r = a^s$. Then

$$a^{s-r} = a^s a^{-r} = a^r a^{-r} = e.$$

Therefore there is at least one positive power, $s - r$, of a which gives the identity element. Let k be the smallest of these powers, so that $a^k = e$.

There is always a smallest power. See Exercise 6A Question 11.

> Let a be an element of a group G. Then a is said to have **finite order** if $a^n = e$ for some positive integer n. The least such n is called the **order** of a.
>
> If no such n exists, the element a has **infinite order**.

'Order' is used quite differently here from its use in the context of 'order of a group'. Some books use the word 'period' instead of 'order' in this context.

Note that, from the definition, in any group the order of the identity e is 1.

Example 6.2.3

Find the orders of the elements of   (a) $(\mathbb{Z}_5, +)$ (b) $(\mathbb{Z}_7 \setminus \{0\}, \times)$,   (c) D_3.

(a)   In $(\mathbb{Z}_5, +)$ use additive notation. The orders of the elements are as follows:

The identity element, 0, has order 1.
As $1 + 1 = 2$, $2 + 1 = 3$, $3 + 1 = 4$, $4 + 1 = 0$, the order of 1 is 4.
As $2 + 2 = 4$, $4 + 2 = 1$, $1 + 2 = 3$, $3 + 2 = 0$, the order of 2 is 4.
As $3 + 3 = 1$, $1 + 3 = 4$, $4 + 3 = 2$, $2 + 3 = 0$, the order of 3 is 4.
As $4 + 4 = 3$, $3 + 4 = 2$, $2 + 4 = 1$, $1 + 4 = 0$, the order of 4 is 4.

(b)   The orders of the elements of $(\mathbb{Z}_7 \setminus \{0\}, \times)$ can be worked out in a similar way:

The identity element, 1, has order 1.
As $2^1 = 2$, $2^2 = 4$, $2^3 = 1$, the order of 2 is 3.
As $3^1 = 3$, $3^2 = 2$, $3^3 = 6$, $3^4 = 4$, $3^5 = 5$, $3^6 = 1$, the order of 3 is 6.
As $4^1 = 4$, $4^2 = 2$, $4^3 = 1$, the order of 4 is 3.
As $5^1 = 5$, $5^2 = 4$, $5^3 = 6$, $5^4 = 2$, $5^5 = 3$, $5^6 = 1$, the order of 5 is 6.
As $6^1 = 6$, $6^2 = 1$, the order of 6 is 2.

(c)   The orders of the elements can be found from the D_3 group table in Table 6.1.

The orders of I, X, Y and Z are respectively $1, 2, 2$ and 2.

Since $R^2 = S$ and $R^3 = RS = I$, the order of R is 3.

Finally $S^2 = R$ and $S^3 = SR = I$, so the order of S is 3.

D_3		First operation performed					
		I	R	S	X	Y	Z
	I	I	R	S	X	Y	Z
Second	R	R	S	I	Z	X	Y
operation	S	S	I	R	Y	Z	X
performed	X	X	Y	Z	I	R	S
	Y	Y	Z	X	S	I	R
	Z	Z	X	Y	R	S	I

Table 6.1

Example 6.2.4

In $(\mathbb{R} \setminus \{0\}, \times)$, give an element of   (a) finite order greater than 1,   (b) infinite order.

(a)   As an element a of finite order has to satisfy the equation $a^n = 1$ and belong to $\mathbb{R} \setminus \{0\}$, the only possibilities are ± 1. Since 1 has order 1 and -1 has order 2, the only example is -1.

(b)   The element 2 has infinite order since $2^n \neq 1$ for any positive integer n.

6.3   Cyclic groups

If G is a group, it is sometimes the case that G consists entirely of the powers of a single element. In this case the group is said to be **generated** by this element.

An example of a finite group of this type is the group of symmetries of an object such as the Manx symbol in Fig. 6.2.

This group consists of the set $\{I, R, R^2\}$, where R is a rotation of $\frac{2}{3}\pi$, together with the operation 'followed by'. Note that R^2, which is a rotation of $-\frac{2}{3}\pi$, is also a generator.

Groups like this are called **cyclic groups**. In the definition of a cyclic group which follows, recall that from the definition of the powers of an element a, $a^0 = e$.

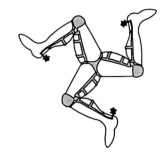

Fig. 6.2

> Let G be a group. If there is an element $a \in G$ such that every element of G has the form a^n for $n \in \mathbb{Z}$, then G is called a **cyclic** group. The element a is called a **generator** for G.

If you can find an element of a group whose order is equal to the order of the group (that is, the number of elements of the group), then it follows that the group is cyclic. One way of showing that a group is not cyclic is to find the order of each element and show that none of them is equal to the order of the group. But there may be simpler ways of showing that a group is not cyclic; for example, if a group is not commutative it can't be cyclic, because all cyclic groups are commutative (why?).

Example 6.3.1
Show that the groups $(\mathbb{Z}_7,+)$ and $(\mathbb{Z}_7 \setminus \{0\},\times)$ are cyclic groups.

To show that $(\mathbb{Z}_7,+)$ is cyclic, you need to interpret the multiplicative notation of the definition of cyclic groups so that you can apply it to a group which uses additive notation.

In $(\mathbb{Z}_7,+)$, 1 is a generator because $1+1=2$, $1+1+1=3$, $1+1+1+1=4$, $1+1+1+1+1=5$, $1+1+1+1+1+1=6$ and $1+1+1+1+1+1+1=0$. As $(\mathbb{Z}_7,+)$ has a generator, it is cyclic.

In $(\mathbb{Z}_7 \setminus \{0\},\times)$, 3 is a generator because its order, 6, is equal to the order of the group (see Example 6.2.3(b)). As $(\mathbb{Z}_7 \setminus \{0\},\times)$ has a generator, it is cyclic.

Note that 5 is also a generator for $(\mathbb{Z}_7 \setminus \{0\},\times)$, but one generator is enough to show it is cyclic.

Example 6.3.2
Show that $(\mathbb{Z},+)$ is a cyclic group.

If an element a is a generator, the group consists of the set of elements $\{...,a^{-3},a^{-2},a^{-1},e,a,a^2,a^3,...\}$. When $a=1$, $a^2=1+1=2$, $a^3=1+1+1=3$ etc., and $a^{-1}=-1$, $a^{-2}=(-1)+(-1)=-2$ etc. Therefore 1 is a generator for $(\mathbb{Z},+)$, and so $(\mathbb{Z},+)$ is a cyclic group.

Note that -1 is also a generator for $(\mathbb{Z},+)$.

Example 6.3.3
Show that the group $(\mathbb{Q}^+,\times)$ is not a cyclic group.

Notice first that 1 is not a generator, since all its powers are 1, and that -1 is not a generator since all its powers are 1 or -1.

Suppose now that x is a generator, where $x \neq 1$ or -1. Then $x^n=-1$ for some value of n, so $\left|x^n\right|=|-1|=1$, giving $|x|^n=1$. But $x \neq 1$ or -1, so this is a contradiction. So $(\mathbb{Q}^+,\times)$ is not a cyclic group.

Exercise 6A

1 Find the powers of 5 in the group G consisting of the elements 1, 2, 4, 5, 7, 8 where $a \circ b$ is the remainder when ab is divided by 9. How many distinct powers of 5 are there?

2 Find the orders of the elements in the groups
  (a) $(\mathbb{Z}_6,+)$,   (b) $(\mathbb{Z}_{11} \setminus \{0\},\times)$,   (c) D_4 (see Exercise 5B Question 3).
  Keep your answer to part (c) for Exercise 6B Question 1.

3 Find all the elements of order 2 in the group of symmetries of a non-square rectangle (see Exercise 5B Question 1.)

4 Find all the elements of order 4 in the group $(\mathbb{C} \setminus \{0\}, \times)$. How many elements of $(\mathbb{C} \setminus \{0\}, \times)$ have order 3?

5 In $(\mathbb{Q} \setminus \{0\}, \times)$, write down all the elements of finite order.

6 Given that the set of non-singular matrices with the operation of matrix multiplication forms a group, show there is an infinite number of elements of order 2.

7 Is the group in Question 1 a cyclic group? Give a reason for your answer.

8 The set $2\mathbb{Z}$ is the set of even integers. Prove that $(2\mathbb{Z}, +)$ is a cyclic group. (You may assume that $(2\mathbb{Z}, +)$ is a group.)

9 The tables below show two groups: one of them is cyclic and one is not. Identify which is which, find all the generators of the cyclic group, and prove that the other group is not cyclic.

	e	a	b	c
e	e	a	b	c
a	a	e	c	b
b	b	c	e	a
c	c	b	a	e

	e	a	b	c
e	e	a	b	c
a	a	b	c	e
b	b	c	e	a
c	c	e	a	b

10 Prove that the groups $(\mathbb{Z}_5, +)$ and $(\mathbb{Z}_6, +)$ are cyclic, and find all their generators.

11* Prove by induction that, in any set of positive integers, there is always a least member.

6.4 Subgroups

Look again at Table 5.5 for the group D_3, reprinted here as Table 6.3 with the title D_3 in the top left corner. Part of the table is shaded; as $S = R^2$, this is the group $\{I, R, R^2\}$ of Fig. 6.2.

D_3	I	R	S	X	Y	Z
I	I	R	S	X	Y	Z
R	R	S	I	Z	X	Y
S	S	I	R	Y	Z	X
X	X	Y	Z	I	R	S
Y	Y	Z	X	S	I	R
Z	Z	X	Y	R	S	I

Table 6.3

The set $\{I, R, S\}$ with the operation 'followed by' is a smaller group inside the whole group; this is called a **subgroup** of D_3.

If you re-drew the table with the elements in the order $\{I, X, R, S, Y, Z\}$ you would find that there is also a small group $\{I, X\}$ in the top left corner. So $\{I, X\}$ is another subgroup of D_3. So too are $\{I, Y\}$ and $\{I, Z\}$.

In addition to these subgroups of D_3, the identity group $\{I\}$, and the whole group $\{I, R, S, X, Y, Z\}$ are also regarded as subgroups of D_3. The subgroups $\{I\}$ and D_3 are called **trivial** subgroups of D_3. The remaining subgroups are called **proper** subgroups of D_3.

> If H is a subset of a group G with operation $\circ$, such that H is a group with operation $\circ$, then H is a **subgroup** of G.
>
> Every group G has two **trivial** subgroups, $\{e\}$ and G itself.
>
> Subgroups of G other than $\{e\}$ and G are called **proper** subgroups.

Example 6.4.1

Explain why $(\mathbb{Q} \setminus \{0\}, \times)$ is not a subgroup of $(\mathbb{Q}, +)$.

Although $\mathbb{Q} \setminus \{0\}$ is a subset of $\mathbb{Q}$, the operations in the two groups are different, so $(\mathbb{Q} \setminus \{0\}, \times)$ is not a subgroup of $(\mathbb{Q}, +)$.

Example 6.4.2

Find all the subgroups of $(\mathbb{Z}_6, +)$, saying which are proper subgroups.

The subgroups are $\{0\}$, $\{0, 3\}$, $\{0, 2, 4, 6\}$ and $\mathbb{Z}_6$ itself. Of these the proper subgroups are $\{0, 3\}$ and $\{0, 2, 4, 6\}$ with the operation of addition modulo 6.

Example 6.4.3

Find a finite proper subgroup and an infinite proper subgroup of $(\mathbb{C} \setminus \{0\}, \times)$.

A finite proper subgroup is $\{1, -1\}$. An infinite proper subgroup is $(\mathbb{R} \setminus \{0\}, \times)$.

Theorem 6.2   Let G be a group, and let H be a non-empty subset of G. Then H is a subgroup of G if

- $a \in H$ and $b \in H \implies ab \in H$
- $e \in H$
- $a \in H \implies a^{-1} \in H$.

Proof

If $a \in H$ and $b \in H \implies ab \in H$, then the operation of G is closed in H.

Suppose that $a, b, c \in H$. Then, since H is a subset of G, $a, b, c \in G$. But the group operation in G is associative, so $(ab)c = a(bc)$. Therefore the operation is associative in H.

Since $ea = ae = a$ for each $a \in G$, $ea = ae = a$ is also true for each $a \in H$.

For $a \in H$, and hence $a^{-1} \in H$, $a^{-1}a = aa^{-1} = e$ because a^{-1} is the inverse of a in G.

Therefore H is a subgroup of G.

Theorem 6.3 shows another way of proving that a non-empty subset H of a group G is a subgroup. It appears easier than the three conditions of Theorem 6.2, but it is less intuitive than Theorem 6.2. Which you decide to use is up to you.

Theorem 6.3   Let G be a group, and let H be a non-empty subset of G. Then H is a subgroup of G if $ab^{-1} \in H$ whenever $a,b \in H$.

Proof

If $a,b \in H \implies ab^{-1} \in H$, then, by writing $b = a$, $aa^{-1} \in H$, so $e \in H$.

If $a,b \in H \implies ab^{-1} \in H$, then, by writing $a = e$ and $b = a^{-1}$,

$$e, a \in H \implies ea^{-1} \in H, \text{ so } a^{-1} \in H. \text{ Similarly, } b^{-1} \in H.$$

So if $a, b^{-1} \in H$, then $a\left(b^{-1}\right)^{-1} \in H$, so $ab \in H$.

The three conditions of Theorem 6.2 hold, so H is a subgroup of G.

Example 6.4.4

Verify that $\left(\mathbb{Z}^+ \cup \{0\}, +\right)$, which satisfies the first two conditions of Theorem 6.2 but not the third, is not a subgroup of $(\mathbb{Z}, +)$.

Since $-1 \notin \left(\mathbb{Z}^+ \cup \{0\}, +\right)$, the element 1 in $\left(\mathbb{Z}^+ \cup \{0\}, +\right)$ has no inverse, so $\left(\mathbb{Z}^+ \cup \{0\}, +\right)$ is not a group and therefore is not a subgroup of $(\mathbb{Z}, +)$.

Example 6.4.5

Prove that $H = \{12x + 21y : x, y \in \mathbb{Z}\}$ is a subgroup of $(\mathbb{Z}, +)$.

As x and y are integers, $12x + 21y$ is an integer, so H is a non-empty subset of $\mathbb{Z}$.

First note that 0 is the identity in $(\mathbb{Z}, +)$ and that $0 = 12 \times 0 + 21 \times 0$ is a member of H.

Method 1   Using Theorem 6.2

If $p, q \in H$, then $p = 12x_1 + 21y_1$ and $q = 12x_2 + 21y_2$ for integers x_1, y_1, x_2 and y_2. So $p + q = (12x_1 + 21y_1) + (12x_2 + 21y_2) = 12(x_1 + x_2) + 21(y_1 + y_2)$ where $x_1 + x_2$ and $y_1 + y_2$ are integers. Therefore $p + q \in H$.

If $p = 12x_1 + 21y_1 \in H$, then $-p = -(12x_1 + 21y_1) = 12(-x_1) + 21(-y_1)$. As $-x_1$ and $-y_1$ are integers, $12(-x_1) + 21(-y_1)$ is also an integer, so $-p \in H$. Also $(-p) + p = p + (-p) = 0$ so $-p$ is the inverse of p. Therefore the inverse of p is a member of H.

Therefore, using Theorem 6.2, H is a subgroup of $(\mathbb{Z}, +)$.

Method 2   Using Theorem 6.3

If $p, q \in H$, then $p = 12x_1 + 21y_1$ and $q = 12x_2 + 21y_2$ for integers x_1, y_1, x_2 and y_2.

Since $0 = 12 \times 0 + 21 \times 0$, and 0 is an integer, $0 \in H$.

If $q = 12x_2 + 21y_2 \in H$, then $-q = -(12x_2 + 21y_2) = 12(-x_2) + 21(-y_2)$. As $-x_2$ and $-y_2$ are integers, $12(-x_2) + 21(-y_2)$ is also an integer, so $-q \in H$. Also $p + (-q) = (-q) + p = 0$ so $-q$ is the inverse of q.

Then $p - q = (12x_1 + 21y_1) + 12(-x_2) + 21(-y_2) = 12(x_1 - x_2) + 21(y_1 - y_2)$ where $x_1 - x_2$ and $y_1 - y_2$ are integers, so $p - q$ is a member of H.

Therefore, using Theorem 6.3, H is a subgroup of $(\mathbb{Z}, +)$.

What is this subgroup? Notice first that any factor of both 12 and 21 divides $12x+21y$, so the highest common factor of 12 and 21, namely 3, divides every member of H.

If you take $x=2$ and $y=-1$, you find that $2\times12+(-1)\times21=3$ is a member of H, so H consists of all multiples of 3.

This argument can be generalised to show that for positive integers a and b, $H=\{ax+by:x,y\in\mathbb{Z}\}$ is a subgroup of $(\mathbb{Z},+)$, and consists of multiples of the highest common factor of a and b.

Subgroups of a finite group

For a finite group G it is usually easy to check from a table whether a subset H is a subgroup. You need only check that the operation on the subset H is closed. For example, in Table 6.3, once you have seen that $\{I,R,S\}$ is closed, you do not need to check the other group properties. This is summarised in the following theorem.

Theorem 6.4 Let G be a group, and let H be a finite subset of G. Then H is a subgroup of G if
$$a\in H \text{ and } b\in H \;\Rightarrow\; ab\in H.$$

Theorem 6.2 proved that any subset H (not necessarily finite) of G which satisfies

- $a\in H$ and $b\in H \Rightarrow ab\in H$
- $e\in H$
- $a\in H \Rightarrow a^{-1}\in H$

is a subgroup. So what remains to be proved is that the first condition, which is given, together with the fact that the set H is finite is sufficient to prove the second and third conditions.

Proof

If, in the statement '$a\in H$ and $b\in H \Rightarrow ab\in H$', you put $a,a^2,a^3,\dots$ in turn instead of b, you find that $a^2\in H$, $a^3\in H$, $a^4\in H$ for all positive powers of a. Using Theorem 6.1, let the order of a be k, so $a^k=e$, and $e\in H$.

Now consider a^{k-1}. Since $a^{k-1}a=a^k=e$, a^{k-1} is the inverse of a. But $a^{k-1}\in H$, so $a^{-1}\in H$.

By Theorem 6.2, H is a subgroup of G.

6.5 The subgroup generated by an element

In D_3 the set of powers of R is $\{R,R^2=S,R^3=I\}$, that is $\{R,S,I\}$, and you saw in Section 6.4 that this is a subgroup of D_3.

Similarly, in $(\mathbb{Z}_7\setminus\{0\},\times)$, the powers of 2 are $\{2,2^2=4,2^3=1\}$ which is a subgroup of $(\mathbb{Z}_7\setminus\{0\},\times)$.

Also, in $(\mathbb{Q},\times)$, the powers of 2, $\{\dots,2^{-s},\dots,2^{-1},1,2,\dots,2^r,\dots\}$, form a subgroup.

In fact, the set of powers of an element is always a subgroup.

Theorem 6.5 Let a be an element of a group G. Then the set of all powers of a, $H=\{a^n:n\in\mathbb{Z}\}$ is a subgroup of G.

Proof

If $p,q\in H$, then $p=a^r$ and $q=a^s$ for integers r and s. Then $pq=a^ra^s=a^{r+s}$, and since $r+s$ is an integer, $pq\in H$.

Since 0 is an integer, $a^0 \in H$. And since $a^0 = e$ by definition, $e \in H$.

If $p \in H$, then $p = a^r$ for an integer r. Therefore $-r$ is an integer, and so $a^{-r} \in H$. But $a^{-r}a^r = a^{r-r} = e$, so a^{-r} is the inverse of p, and belongs to H.

Therefore $H = \left\{ a^n : n \in \mathbb{Z} \right\}$ is a subgroup of G.

This proof applies to both finite and infinite groups.

> The subgroup H of a group G defined by $H = \left\{ a^n : n \in \mathbb{Z} \right\}$ is said to be the subgroup **generated** by a.

If an element a has infinite order, then the group generated by a is $\left\{ ..., a^{-2}, a^{-1}, e, a, a^2, ... \right\}$ and is infinite.

If an element a has finite order n, then the group generated by a is $\left\{ e, a, a^2, ..., a^{n-1} \right\}$. The order of the subgroup generated by a is then the same as the order of a.

Notice that the subgroup generated by an element is a cyclic subgroup, and that the order of the cyclic subgroup is the same as the order of the generating element.

Exercise 6B

1 (a) Find the orders of the elements of the group D_4 (see Exercise 6A Question 2(c)).

(b) Find the cyclic subgroups of D_4.

(c) Find two proper non-cyclic subgroups of D_4.

2 Find all the subgroups of   (a) $(\mathbb{Z}_4, +)$,   (b) $(\mathbb{Z}_5, +)$.

3 Find all the proper subgroups of S_3 (see Table 5.9).

4 Find a finite subgroup, apart from $\{1\}$, of the group $(\mathbb{R} \setminus \{0\}, \times)$.

5 Prove that the set $(\{..., -3n, -2n, -n, 0, n, 2n, 3n, ...\}, +)$, where $n \in \mathbb{N}$, is a cyclic group.

6 Show that the group of functions $\left\{ x \mapsto ax \mid a \in \mathbb{R}, a \neq 0 \right\}$ is a subgroup of the group $\left\{ x \mapsto ax + b \mid a, b \in \mathbb{R}, a \neq 0 \right\}$ under the operation of composition of functions.

7 Prove that if G is cyclic it is commutative.

8 Let G be a group, and let g be a fixed element of G. Prove that the set of elements which commute with g, that is $H = \{ x \in G : gx = xg \}$ is a subgroup of G. Identify H in the following examples.

(a) G is D_3 and g is R.

(b) G is D_3 and g is X.

(c) G is the set of 2×2 matrices under multiplication and g is $\begin{pmatrix} 1 & 1 \\ 0 & 1 \end{pmatrix}$.

(d) G is Q_4 (see Question 9) and g is q.

(e) G is A_4 (see Question 10) and g is x.

9 Find all the subgroups of the quaternion group denoted by Q_4, shown in the table. Keep a note of their orders for the next section.

Q_4	e	a	b	c	p	q	r	s
e	e	a	b	c	p	q	r	s
a	a	b	c	e	s	p	q	r
b	b	c	e	a	r	s	p	q
c	c	e	a	b	q	r	s	p
p	p	q	r	s	b	c	e	a
q	q	r	s	p	a	b	c	e
r	r	s	p	q	e	a	b	c
s	s	p	q	r	c	e	a	b

10 The group A_4 of rotational symmetries of the regular tetrahedron has order 12 and is shown in the table below. Find all the subgroups, and make a note of their orders for the next section. Check that A_4 has no subgroup of order 6.

A_4	e	a	b	c	x	y	z	t	p	q	r	s
e	e	a	b	c	x	y	z	t	p	q	r	s
a	a	e	c	b	z	t	x	y	s	r	q	p
b	b	c	e	a	t	z	y	x	q	p	s	r
c	c	b	a	e	y	x	t	z	r	s	p	q
x	x	t	y	z	p	s	q	r	e	c	a	b
y	y	z	x	t	r	q	s	p	c	e	b	a
z	z	y	t	x	s	p	r	q	a	b	e	c
t	t	x	z	y	q	r	p	s	b	a	c	e
p	p	r	s	q	e	b	c	a	x	z	t	y
q	q	s	r	p	b	e	a	c	t	y	x	z
r	r	p	q	s	c	a	e	b	y	t	z	x
s	s	q	p	r	a	c	b	e	z	x	y	t

6.6 Lagrange's theorem

If you look back at some of the results of Exercise 6B in which you found subgroups of finite groups, and at the examples before Exercise 6B, you find that

- the subgroups of D_3, which has order 6, have orders 1, 2, 3 and 6
- the subgroups of $(\mathbb{Z}_4, +)$, which has order 4, have orders 1, 2 and 4
- the subgroups of $(\mathbb{Z}_5, +)$, which has order 5, have orders 1 and 5
- the subgroups of D_4, which has order 8, have orders 1, 2, 4 and 8
- the subgroups of Q_4, which has order 8, have orders 1, 2, 4 and 8
- the subgroups of A_4, which has order 12, have orders 1, 2, 3, 4 and 12.

You have enough evidence to conjecture that, for finite groups, the order of a subgroup divides the order of the group. This result is called Lagrange's theorem after Joseph-Louis Lagrange (1736–1813).

> **Lagrange's theorem**   Let H be a subgroup of a finite group G. Then the order of H divides the order of G.

Lagrange's theorem is proved in Section 6.7.

Lagrange's theorem has a number of immediate consequences, called **corollaries**.

Corollary 1   The order of an element of a finite group G divides the order of G.

The order of an element a is equal to the order of the subgroup generated by a.

By Lagrange's theorem, the order of a divides the order of the group.

Corollary 2   A group of prime order has no proper subgroups.

If the order of a group G is a prime number, p, by Lagrange's theorem the only possible subgroups will have orders 1 and p.

But these subgroups will be the trivial subgroups consisting of the identity only and the whole group.

Therefore there are no proper subgroups.

Corollary 3   Every group G of prime order p is cyclic.

Consider an element $a \in G$ other than the identity.

As the order of a divides p, and a is not the identity, the order of a must be p itself.

Therefore a is a generator for G, and G is cyclic.

It is tempting to think that the converse of Lagrange's theorem might be true, that if the order of a finite group G has a factor n, then there is a subgroup of G with order n; but this is actually false. A_4, the group with 12 elements in Exercise 6B Question 10, has no subgroup of order 6.

Exercise 6C

1 Use Lagrange's theorem to state the possible orders of subgroups of a group of order 24.

2 Explain why a group of order 15 cannot have a subgroup of order 9.

3 G is a finite cyclic group of order pq, where p and q are prime. What are the possible orders of subgroups of G?

4 Prove that the order of a finite group with at least two elements but no proper subgroups is prime.

5 Let p be a prime number. What are the possible orders of subgroups of $\mathbb{Z}_p \times \mathbb{Z}_p$ and $\mathbb{Z}_p \times \mathbb{Z}_{p^2}$?

6.7* Proof of Lagrange's theorem

You may, if you wish, omit this section.

Let H be a subgroup of a finite group G. The idea of the proof of Lagrange's theorem is to show that the elements of the finite group G can be parcelled up into separate packages, called cosets, one of which is the subgroup H itself. It will turn out that all these packages have the same number of elements as H. Lagrange's theorem then follows easily.

If $a \in G$, then the set $Ha = \{ha : h \in H\}$ is called a **right coset** of H in G.

Example 6.7.1

Find the right cosets of the subgroup $\{I, X\}$ in D_3.

To find the right cosets, write out part of the group table of D_3 with the elements of the subgroup $\{I, X\}$ in the top places in the left column, as shown in Table 6.4.

	I	R	S	X	Y	Z
I	I	R	S	X	Y	Z
X	X	Y	Z	I	R	S

Table 6.4

Each column of the table is a right coset of the subgroup $\{I, X\}$ in D_3.

To see that this is true, notice that the first column consists of the subgroup multiplied on the right by I; the second column consists of the elements $IR = R$ and $XR = Y$, that is the elements I and X of the subgroup $\{I, X\}$ multiplied on the right by R; and so on.

Recall that, as the order in which the elements of a set are written is irrelevant, the set $\{I, X\}$ is the same as the set $\{X, I\}$. Similarly $\{R, Y\} = \{Y, R\}$ and $\{S, Z\} = \{Z, S\}$.

There are three distinct right cosets: $\{I, X\}$, $\{R, Y\}$ and $\{S, Z\}$.

Notice that the elements of the group are divided equally among three cosets.

Example 6.7.2

The group Q_4, called the quaternion group, is shown in Table 6.5. Find the right cosets of the subgroups $H_1 = \{e, b\}$ and $H_2 = \{e, a, b, c\}$.

Q_4	e	a	b	c	p	q	r	s
e	e	a	b	c	p	q	r	s
a	a	b	c	e	s	p	q	r
b	b	c	e	a	r	s	p	q
c	c	e	a	b	q	r	s	p
p	p	q	r	s	b	c	e	a
q	q	r	s	p	a	b	c	e
r	r	s	p	q	e	a	b	c
s	s	p	q	r	c	e	a	b

Table 6.5

Proceed as in Example 6.7.1, and write out just those rows of the group table for Q_4 which contain the elements of the subgroup in the column on the left. This is shown in Table 6.6.

	e	a	b	c	p	q	r	s
e	e	a	b	c	p	q	r	s
b	b	c	e	a	r	s	p	q

Table 6.6

The right cosets of H_1 are $\{e,b\}$, $\{a,c\}$, $\{p,r\}$ and $\{q,s\}$.

Working in the same way with the subgroup $H_2 = \{e,a,b,c\}$ gives Table 6.7.

	e	a	b	c	p	q	r	s
e	e	a	b	c	p	q	r	s
a	a	b	c	e	s	p	q	r
b	b	c	e	a	r	s	p	q
c	c	e	a	b	q	r	s	p

Table 6.7

The right cosets of H_2 are $\{e,a,b,c\}$ and $\{p,q,r,s\}$.

Notice that, for both H_1 and H_2, the order of the subgroup multiplied by the number of cosets gives the order of the group.

Lagrange's theorem follows from the three parts of the following theorem.

Theorem 6.6   Let H be a subgroup of a finite group G. Then

(a) any two right cosets of H in G are either identical or have no elements in common,
(b) all the right cosets of H in G have the same number of elements,
(c) every element of G is in some right coset of H in G.

Proof

(a)   Let a and b be elements of G. Then either b belongs to Ha, or it doesn't.

Case 1 b belongs to Ha. Then $b = ha$ for some $h \in H$. Let x be any element of Hb. Then $x = h_1 b = h_1 ha = h_2 a$, where $h_2 \in H$, since H is a subgroup. But $h_2 a \in Ha$, so $x \in Ha$, and all the elements of Hb are members of Ha.

Case 2 b does not belong to Ha. Then no element of Hb belongs to Ha, since if $h_1 b = h_2 a$, then $b = h_1^{-1} h_2 a = h_3 a$ where $h_3 \in H$, a contradiction.

So either all elements of Hb are in Ha or no elements of Hb are in Ha. Now notice the symmetrical roles of a and b, in the sense that you could also prove that either all elements of Ha are in Hb or no elements of Ha are in Hb. Thus any two right cosets of H in G are either identical or have no elements in common.

(b) G is finite, so H is finite. Let H have n elements, $H = \{h_1, h_2, \ldots, h_n\}$. Then the elements of Ha are $\{h_1 a, h_2 a, \ldots, h_n a\}$. No two of these are the same, since if $h_r a = h_s a$ then $h_r = h_s$ by the cancellation law; so Ha also has n elements. So every right coset of H has n elements.

(c)   Let a be any element of G. Then the coset Ha contains a because $e \in H$ and you can write $a = ea$.

All the bricks are now to hand to prove Lagrange's theorem.

Theorem 6.7 (Lagrange's theorem)   Let H be a subgroup of a finite group G. Then the order of H divides the order of G.

Proof

Let G and H have orders m and n respectively. Then by Theorem 6.6(b), each right coset of H has exactly n elements.

By Theorem 6.6(a), any two of the right cosets either are identical or have no elements in common. Suppose that there are d distinct cosets.

These d cosets therefore account for nd elements of the group G. But part (c) of Theorem 6.6 states that every element of the group is in some coset, so these nd elements account for all the elements of the group. Thus $nd = m$, so n divides m.

Therefore the order of H divides the order of G.

Exercise 6D*

1 Find the right cosets of the subgroups $\{I, R, S\}$, $\{I\}$ and D_3 itself in the group D_3.

2 Find the right cosets of $\{0, 3\}$ in $(\mathbb{Z}_6, +)$. (You will have to use additive notation.)

3 The table in Exercise 6B Question 10 shows the group A_4, the symmetry group of the tetrahedron. Find the right cosets of

   (a) $H_1 = \{e, a, b, c\}$,   (b) the subgroup H_2 generated by x.

4 Find the right cosets of the subgroup $\{0, \pm 3, \pm 6, \ldots\}$ of the group $(\mathbb{Z}, +)$.

7 Isomorphisms of groups

This chapter is about groups that are identical to each other as regards their structure. When you have completed it, you should

- know what is meant by isomorphic groups or an isomorphism between groups
- know all the different (non-isomorphic) groups with orders up to 7.

7.1 What are isomorphic groups?

The word 'isomorphic' literally means 'equal in form'. When the word is applied to a pair of groups it means that the groups are structurally the same as each other.

For example, consider the groups $(\mathbb{Z}_4, +)$ and $(\{1, i, -1, -i\}, \times)$ in Tables 7.1 and 7.2.

+	0	1	2	3
0	0	1	2	3
1	1	2	3	0
2	2	3	0	1
3	3	0	1	2

Table 7.1

×	1	i	-1	-i
1	1	i	-1	-i
i	i	-1	-i	1
-1	-1	-i	1	i
-i	-i	1	i	-1

Table 7.2

You can see that these tables, apart from their labelling, are identical. The symbol 1 appears in Table 7.2 in every place that the symbol 0 appears in Table 7.1. Similarly i appears in place of 1, −1 appears in place of 2 and −i in place of 3.

Groups with tables that are related in this way are said to be **isomorphic** to each other. In applying this statement, however, you need to take care. Table 7.3 shows the group $(\{2, 4, 6, 8\}, \times (\mathrm{mod}\,10))$.

×(mod 10)	2	4	6	8
2	4	8	2	6
4	8	6	4	2
6	2	4	6	8
8	6	2	8	4

Table 7.3

×(mod 10)	6	2	4	8
6	6	2	4	8
2	2	4	8	6
4	4	8	6	2
8	8	6	2	4

Table 7.4

You might think that the group defined by this table is not isomorphic to $(\mathbb{Z}_4, +)$, but in fact, it is. The group identity is 6, so try rearranging the elements as in Table 7.4, so that they are in the order 6, 2, 4, 8, with the group identity first. You can now see, by comparing Table 7.4 with Table 7.1, that the group *is* isomorphic to $(\mathbb{Z}_4, +)$.

So tables can be helpful for detecting isomorphisms between small groups, but you must not be misled by the way the elements are arranged in the table. For larger groups, tables are cumbersome to use. For infinite groups, tables cannot be used at all.

However, you can use tables to develop a general definition of isomorphism of groups G and H. The important idea is that to every $a \in G$ in Table 7.5, there corresponds an $A \in H$ in Table 7.6. Moreover, if an element x in G is the product of two elements a and b, that is $x = ab$, an X must appear in the corresponding position in H, as the product of the image of a and the image of b, that is $X = AB$.

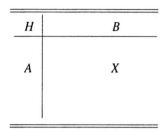

G	b
a	x

Table 7.5

H	B
A	X

Table 7.6

The language of the previous paragraph should remind you of the language of functions in Chapter 3.

Looking again at Tables 7.5 and 7.6, and the paragraph above them, you can define a function $f : G \to H$, such that $f(a) = A$, $f(b) = B$ and $f(x) = X$. You can now write the condition $X = AB$ as $f(x) = f(a)f(b)$, and since $x = ab$, it follows that $f(ab) = f(a)f(b)$.

7.2 A definition of isomorphism

In addition to the condition that $f(ab) = f(a)f(b)$ you would also expect isomorphic finite groups to have the same order. You can make sure that this happens by imposing two conditions: by allowing no spare elements in H which are not the images of elements in G, that is, f is a surjection; and by requiring that different elements of G be sent to different elements of H, that is, f is an injection. Note that since f is both an injection and a surjection, it is a bijection (see Section 3.4). Summarising:

> Two groups $(G, \circ)$ and $(H, *)$ are **isomorphic** if there exists a function
> $f : G \to H$ such that
>
> - f is a bijection
> - $f(a \circ b) = f(a) * f(b)$ for all $a, b \in G$.
>
> The function $f : G \to H$ is called an **isomorphism**.

The definition looks oddly asymmetrical between the two groups G and H, but it isn't really. If you write $f^{-1} = F$, the definition could be reversed in terms of F by writing $F : H \to G$, with $F(A * B) = F(A)F(B) = a \circ b$.

It is usual to drop the group operation symbols $\circ$ and $*$, and to use multiplicative notation for both groups. Then $f(a \circ b) = f(a) * f(b)$ becomes $f(ab) = f(a)f(b)$.

It is comforting that many of the things that you would expect to be true about isomorphic groups are indeed true.

Here are three important examples.

Theorem 7.1   If $f : G \to H$ is an isomorphism of G and H, and e is the identity in G, then $f(e)$ is the identity in H. If $a \in G$, then $f\left(a^{-1}\right)$ is the inverse of $f(a)$ in H.

You must expect to use the relation $f(ab) = f(a)f(b)$ somewhere in this proof.

Proof
Let e be the identity in G.

If $a \in G$, then

$$f(e)f(a) = f(ea) \qquad \text{(using } f(ab) = f(a)f(b)\text{)}$$
$$= f(a) \qquad (e \text{ is the identity in } G)$$

and

$$f(a)f(e) = f(ae) \qquad \text{(using } f(ab) = f(a)f(b)\text{)}$$
$$= f(a). \qquad (e \text{ is the identity in } G)$$

Therefore $f(e)f(a) = f(a)f(e) = f(a)$, so $f(e)$ is the identity in H. Call it e_H.

To prove that $f\left(a^{-1}\right)$ is the inverse of $f(a)$, you must prove that

$$f\left(a^{-1}\right)f(a) = f(a)f\left(a^{-1}\right) = e_H .$$

Starting with $f\left(a^{-1}\right)f(a)$, you find that

$$f\left(a^{-1}\right)f(a) = f\left(a^{-1}a\right) \qquad \text{(using } f(ab) = f(a)f(b)\text{)}$$
$$= f(e) \qquad (\text{as } a^{-1}a = e)$$
$$= e_H . \qquad (\text{already proved})$$

Similarly, $f(a)f\left(a^{-1}\right) = e_H$, so $f(a)f\left(a^{-1}\right) = f\left(aa^{-1}\right) = f(e) = e_H$ and the theorem is proved.

Theorem 7.2   If $f : G \to H$ is an isomorphism of G and H, the order of the element $a \in G$ is the same as the order of $f(a) \in H$.

Proof
Let n be the order of a. Then n is the smallest positive integer such that $a^n = e$. Consider

$$(f(a))^n = \overbrace{f(a)f(a)\ldots f(a)}^{n \text{ of these}} \qquad \text{(by definition of } n\text{th power)}$$
$$= f(aa\ldots a) \qquad \text{(using } f(ab) = f(a)f(b)\text{)}$$
$$= f\left(a^n\right) \qquad \text{(by definition of } n\text{th power)}$$
$$= f(e) \qquad \text{(the order of } a \text{ is } n)$$
$$= e_H .$$

But is n the *least* positive integer such that $(f(a))^n = e_H$?

Suppose that the order of $f(a)$ is m where $m < n$. Then $(f(a))^m = e_H$.

As $f\left(a^m\right) = (f(a))^m = e_H$, there are two elements, a^n and a^m, with image e_H.

But $a^n \neq a^m$, since $a^n = e$ and n is the smallest positive integer such that $a^n = e$ and $m < n$.

This contradicts the fact that the isomorphism $f : G \to H$ is one-to-one.

Therefore the order of $a \in G$ is the same as the order of $f(a) \in H$.

This theorem is particularly useful for proving that two groups are not isomorphic. Just look at the elements of each group and find their orders. If they don't match, the groups are not isomorphic.

The converse of this result is false. You can have two groups G and H of the same order and set up a function $f : G \to H$ such that the range of f is H, f is one-to-one and elements of G and their images in H have the same orders, but G and H are not isomorphic. The order of the lowest example is 16.

Example 7.2.1
Prove that $(\mathbb{Z}_6, +)$ is not isomorphic to D_3.

The elements $0, 1, 2, 3, 4, 5 \in \mathbb{Z}_6$ have orders $1, 6, 3, 2, 3, 6$ respectively.

The elements $I, R, R^2, X, Y, Z \in D_3$ have orders $1, 3, 3, 2, 2, 2$ respectively.

Therefore the groups are not isomorphic.

Example 7.2.2
Prove that $(\mathbb{R}, +)$ is not isomorphic to $(\mathbb{C} \setminus \{0\}, \times)$.

The only element of finite order in $(\mathbb{R}, +)$ is 0, which has order 1. In $(\mathbb{C} \setminus \{0\}, \times)$ the element -1 has order 2. Therefore the groups are not isomorphic.

Theorem 7.3   (a) Every infinite cyclic group is isomorphic to $(\mathbb{Z}, +)$.
(b) Every finite cyclic group of order n is isomorphic to $(\mathbb{Z}_n, +)$.

To prove that two groups are isomorphic, produce a function from the first group to the second, and show that the function is an isomorphism.

Proof
For both parts (a) and (b), the method is to take a generator a of the cyclic group G, and to define a function $f : \mathbb{Z} \to G$ or $f : \mathbb{Z}_n \to G$ such that $f(r) = a^r$. Then every element of G is the image of some element of $\mathbb{Z}$ or $\mathbb{Z}_n$, so that the range of f is G.

(a)   **Infinite case**
To prove that f is injective, suppose that $f(r) = f(s)$ with $r > s$.

Then $a^r = a^s$, so $a^{r-s} = e$ for $r - s \neq 0$.

But this contradicts the fact that G is an infinite cyclic group, so f is injective.

To prove that $f(r + s) = f(r)f(s)$, consider first $f(r + s) = a^{r+s}$.

But $a^{r+s} = a^r a^s = f(r)f(s)$, so $f : \mathbb{Z} \to G$ is an isomorphism.

(b)   **Finite case**

Let the order of G be n. Define $f : \mathbb{Z}_n \to G$ by $f(r) = a^r$ for $0 \leq r < n$.

To prove that f is injective, suppose that $f(r) = f(s)$ with $r > s$.

Then $a^r = a^s$, so $a^{r-s} = e$.

But as $0 \leq s < r < n$, then $0 < r - s < n$, which contradicts the fact that n is the order of G.

Therefore f is injective.

Finally, to prove that $f(r + s) = a^{r+s}$ there are two cases to consider. Notice first that $0 \leq r + s < 2n$, so that either $0 \leq r + s < n$ or $n \leq r + s < 2n$.

If $0 \leq r + s < n$, then $f(r + s) = a^{r+s} = a^r a^s = f(r)f(s)$.

However, if $n \leq r + s < 2n$, then the sum of r and s in $\mathbb{Z}_n$ is $r + s - n$, so

$$f(r + s) = f(r + s - n) = a^{r+s-n} = a^r a^s e = a^r a^s = f(r)f(s).$$

Therefore $f : \mathbb{Z}_n \to G$ is an isomorphism.

This theorem says that cyclic groups of a given order are isomorphic. This is sometimes stated as, 'there is only one cyclic group of a given order, up to isomorphism'.

Example 7.2.3

Prove that the following groups are isomorphic to each other.

(a) Rotational symmetries of a wheel with 10 equally spaced spokes
(b) $(\mathbb{Z}_{11} \setminus \{0\}, \times)$
(c) $(\mathbb{Z}_{10}, +)$
(d) 10th roots of unity under multiplication

The groups are all cyclic. Possible generators are (a) rotation through $\frac{1}{5}\pi$, (b) 2, (c) 1, (d) $\exp\left(\frac{1}{5}\pi i\right)$.

The groups all have 10 elements, so they are isomorphic.

Example 7.2.4

Prove that the subgroup $\{0, \pm 2, \pm 4, \pm 6, \ldots\}$ of $(\mathbb{Z}, +)$ is isomorphic to $(\mathbb{Z}, +)$.

Method 1   The subgroup $\{0, \pm 2, \pm 4, \pm 6, \ldots\}$ is infinite, and 2 is a generator, so by Theorem 7.3(a) it is isomorphic to $(\mathbb{Z}, +)$.

Method 2   Consider the function $f : \mathbb{Z} \to \{0, \pm 2, \pm 4, \pm 6, \ldots\}$ defined by $f(n) = 2n$.

To prove that f is injective, suppose that $f(i) = f(j)$. Then $2i = 2j$, so $i = j$.

To prove that f is surjective, suppose that there is an element $n \in \{0, \pm 2, \pm 4, \pm 6, \ldots\}$ which is not the image of an element of $\mathbb{Z}$. Since $n \in \{0, \pm 2, \pm 4, \pm 6, \ldots\}$ this element is of the form $n = 2m$ for some integer m, so $f(m) = 2m = n$, and f is surjective.

Hence f is an injection and a surjection, and so it is a bijection.

Finally, $f(i + j) = 2(i + j) = 2i + 2j = f(i) + f(j)$, so f is an isomorphism.

Exercise 7A

1. Show that the group $(\{1,-1\},\times)$ is isomorphic to $(\mathbb{Z}_2,+)$.

2. Use the function $f(x)=e^x$ to show that $(\mathbb{R},+)$ is isomorphic to $(\mathbb{R}^+,\times)$.

3. Show that $(\mathbb{Z}_{13}\setminus\{0\},\times(\text{mod}\,13))$ is isomorphic to $(\mathbb{Z}_{12},+)$.

4. Prove that the group of even integers under addition is isomorphic to the group of integers under addition.

5. Prove that $(\mathbb{R}\setminus\{0\},\times)$ is not isomorphic to $(\mathbb{C}\setminus\{0\},\times)$.

6. Let g be a fixed element of the group G. Prove that $f:G\to G$ defined by $f(a)=g^{-1}ag$ is an isomorphism from G to itself.

7.3 Group generators

You met the idea of a group generator in the context of cyclic groups in Section 6.3. However, you can extend the idea to non-cyclic groups.

Consider the group of symmetries of a rectangle which is not a square. The individual symmetries are the identity e, the reflections a and b in the axes of symmetry, and the rotation of $180°$ about the centre, which you can obtain by carrying out either first a then b or first b then a. In fact, you can describe this group by saying that it is generated by a and b given that $a^2=b^2=e$ and $ab=ba$. You can then simplify any expression in a and b, such as bab^2aba^2 by moving all the b terms to the left using the relation $ab=ba$ to get b^4a^4. Using $a^2=b^2=e$ simplifies this to e.

Similarly, the group D_3 is generated by R and X. A copy of D_3 (from Table 5.5) is shown in Table 7.7 on the next page. Notice first that $S=R^2$, $Y=XR$, $Z=XS=XR^2$ and $R^3=X^2=I$, so that every element can be written in terms of R and X. But notice also that the two equations $XR=Y$ and $R^2X=SX=Y$ give the relation $XR=R^2X$ between R and X.

These relations are sufficient to carry out any calculations within the group.

Now consider XR^2.

$$XR^2=(XR)R=(R^2X)R=R^2(XR)=R^2(R^2X)=R^4X=RX.$$

You can construct a table for D_3 using only R and X. The entries shown in Table 7.8 are easy to supply. These entries come from calculations such as

$$(XR)(XR^2)=X(RX)R^2=X(XR^2)R^2=X^2R^4=R,$$

and

$$(R^2)(XR)=(R^2X)R=(XR)R=XR^2,$$

in which the terms in X are progressively moved to the left using the given relation $XR=R^2X$ and the relation $RX=XR^2$, which was derived from it. Try filling in the rest of Table 7.8 for yourself.

D_3	I	R	S	X	Y	Z
I	I	R	S	X	Y	Z
R	R	S	I	Z	X	Y
S	S	I	R	Y	Z	X
X	X	Y	Z	I	R	S
Y	Y	Z	X	S	I	R
Z	Z	X	Y	R	S	I

Table 7.7

	I	R	R^2	X	XR	XR^2
I	I	R	R^2	X	XR	XR^2
R	R	R^2	I			
R^2	R^2	I	R			
X	X	XR	XR^2	I		
XR	XR	XR^2	X		I	
XR^2	XR^2	X	XR			I

Table 7.8

Thus the group D_3 is generated by R and X where $R^3 = X^2 = I$ and $XR = R^2X$.

In the next section, the idea of generators will be used extensively.

7.4 Classifying groups of order up to 7

The only group of order 1 is the group consisting of the identity element only.

As every group of prime order is cyclic (Section 6.6) the only groups of orders 2, 3, 5 and 7 are cyclic.

This leaves groups of orders 4 and 6. They need a much more detailed treatment.

Groups of order 4

Let G be a group of order 4. As the orders of the elements must divide the order of the group, all the elements of G, other than the identity, have order 4 or 2.

If there is an element of order 4, the group G is cyclic, and is isomorphic to $(\mathbb{Z}_4, +)$.

If there is no element of order 4, all the elements other than the identity have order 2.

Now an element of order 2 is its own inverse; that is, $a^2 = e \Leftrightarrow a = a^{-1}$. Recall from Example 6.1.1 that a group in which every element is its own inverse is commutative.

Let a and b be two distinct non-identity elements of G, and consider the element ba.

As the group is commutative, $ba = ab$.

At this stage the group table shown in Table 7.9 is incomplete.

	e	a	b
e	e	a	b
a	a	e	
b	b	ba	e

Table 7.9

	e	a	b	ba
e	e	a	b	ba
a	a	e	ba	b
b	b	ba	e	a
ba	ba	b	a	e

Table 7.10

The element ba in Table 7.9, shown shaded, cannot be b or e because b and e are already in the same row. And it cannot be a since a is in the same column. So ba is distinct from the other elements, and $G = \{e, a, b, ba\}$.

Complete the table for yourself using similar arguments. You should end up with Table 7.10.

This group is called the four-group or occasionally the Klein four-group. It is denoted by V after the German word *vier* meaning 'four'. It is isomorphic to the group of symmetries of the rectangle. See Exercise 5B Question 1.

There are thus two, and only two, distinct groups of order 4, the cyclic group $(\mathbb{Z}_4, +)$, and V. Every group of order 4 is isomorphic to one of them.

Groups of order 6
Let G be a group of order 6. As the orders of the elements must divide the order of the group, all the elements of G, other than the identity, have order 6, 3 or 2.

If there is an element of order 6, the group G is cyclic, and is isomorphic to $(\mathbb{Z}_6, +)$.

If there is no element of order 6, suppose that there is an element a of order 3. Then the group includes the elements e, a and a^2, and there must be another element b such that $b \neq e$, a or a^2. Thus the elements of G are $\{e, a, a^2, b, ba, ba^2\}$. It is easy to check that none of these six elements can be equal to one another.

At this stage the incomplete group table appears as in Table 7.11.

	e	a	a^2	b	ba	ba^2
e	e	a	a^2	b	ba	ba^2
a	a	a^2	e			
a^2	a^2	e	a			
b	b	ba	ba^2			
ba	ba	ba^2	b			
ba^2	ba^2	b	ba			

Table 7.11

Now consider b^2. It is in the same row as b, ba and ba^2, so it can't be any of them. This leaves only $b^2 = a$, $b^2 = a^2$ or $b^2 = e$ as possibilities.

Suppose first that $b^2 = a$. Then $b^3 = b(b^2) = ba$, $b^4 = b(b^3) = b(ba) = b^2a = a^2$, $b^5 = b(b^4) = ba^2$ and $b^6 = b(b^5) = b(ba^2) = b^2a^2 = aa^2 = a^3 = e$. As these powers of b are all different, the order of b would be 6, contrary to hypothesis.

A similar argument shows that if $b^2 = a^2$, the order of b would also be 6. Try it!

Therefore $b^2 = e$.

Now consider the product ab. It is in the same row as a, a^2 and e and in the same column as b, so it can't be any of them. That leaves two cases, $ab = ba$ and $ab = ba^2$.

Suppose $ab = ba$ and consider the various powers of ab:

$$(ab)^2 = abab = a(ba)b = aabb = a^2b^2 = a^2e = a^2,$$

$$(ab)^3 = (ab)^2 ab = a^2ab = a^3b = b, \qquad\qquad (ab)^4 = (ab)^2(ab)^2 = a^2a^2 = a,$$

$$(ab)^5 = (ab)^3(ab)^2 = ba^2, \qquad\qquad (ab)^6 = (ab)^2(ab)^4 = a^2a = a^3 = e.$$

So the order of ab is 6, contrary to hypothesis. Thus $ab \neq ba$.

If $ab = ba^2$, you can construct a table, using computations such as

$$\left(ba^2\right)(ba) = ba^2ba = ba(ab)a = baba^2a = bab = bba^2 = a^2;$$

$$(ba)\left(ba^2\right) = baba^2 = b(ab)a^2 = bba^2a^2 = b^2a^4 = a.$$

Complete the table for yourself. You should get the result shown in Table 7.12.

	e	a	a^2	b	ba	ba^2
e	e	a	a^2	b	ba	ba^2
a	a	a^2	e	ba^2	b	ba
a^2	a^2	e	a	ba	ba^2	b
b	b	ba	ba^2	e	a	a^2
ba	ba	ba^2	b	a^2	e	a
ba^2	ba^2	b	ba	a	a^2	e

Table 7.12

Comparing Table 7.12 with the completed version of Table 7.8, you can easily see that this group is isomorphic to the group D_3.

Suppose now that G has no elements of order 6 or of order 3. Then all the elements other than the identity have order 2, and the group is commutative (see Example 6.1.1).

Then, if a and b are two distinct, non-identity elements in G, the argument goes precisely as for the non-cyclic group of order 4: G contains e, a, b and ba, but there are no more products of a and b with results distinct from these. But $\{e,a,b,ab\}$ is V, a group of order 4 and, by Lagrange's theorem, a group of order 6 cannot have a subgroup of order 4. So the supposition that all the elements have order 2 leads to a contradiction.

Therefore the only distinct groups of order 6 are $(\mathbb{Z}_6, +)$ and D_3. Every group of order 6 is isomorphic to one or the other of them.

The groups of order up to and including 7 are

$(\mathbb{Z}_2, +)$ of order 2, $(\mathbb{Z}_3, +)$ of order 3, $(\mathbb{Z}_4, +)$ and V of order 4,

$(\mathbb{Z}_5, +)$ of order 5, $(\mathbb{Z}_6, +)$ and D_3 of order 6, $(\mathbb{Z}_7, +)$ of order 7.

Exercise 7B

1 The set $\{2,4,6,8\}$ forms a group G under multiplication modulo 10.

(a) Write down the operation table for G.

(b) State the identity element and the inverse of each element in G.

The set $\{1,i,-1,-i\}$, where $i^2 = -1$, forms a group H under multiplication of complex numbers.

(c) Determine whether or not G and H are isomorphic, giving a reason for your answer.   (OCR)

2 A group D, of order 8, has the operation table shown below.

	e	a	b	b^2	b^3	ab	ab^2	ab^3
e	e	a	b	b^2	b^3	ab	ab^2	ab^3
a	a	e	ab	ab^2	ab^3	b	b^2	b^3
b	b	ab^3	b^2	b^3	e	a	ab	ab^2
b^2	b^2	ab^2	b^3	e	b	ab^3	a	ab
b^3	b^3	ab	e	b	b^2	ab^2	ab^3	a
ab	ab	b^3	ab^2	ab^3	a	e	b	b^2
ab^2	ab^2	b^2	ab^3	a	ab	b^3	e	b
ab^3	ab^3	b	a	ab	ab^2	b^2	b^3	e

(a) Find the orders of the eight elements of D.

(b) Write down the number of subgroups of order 2.

(c) Find two subgroups of order 4.

(d) Give a reason why there is no subgroup of order 6.

(e) Explain how you can tell that the group D is not isomorphic to the group M, in which the elements $\{1,3,7,9,11,13,17,19\}$ are combined by multiplication modulo 20.   (OCR)

3 (a) The set S consists of the eight elements 9^1, 9^2, ... , 9^8 written in arithmetic modulo 64. Determine each of the elements of S as an integer between 0 and 63.

Under multiplication modulo 64, the set S forms a group G, with identity 1. Write down the orders of each of the remaining elements of G.

Write down all the possible generators for G, and list all the subgroups of G.

(b) The group H consists of the set $\{1,9,31,39,41,49,71,79\}$ under multiplication modulo 80. Determine, with justification, whether G and H are isomorphic.   (OCR)

4 The set $S = \{1,2,p,q,7,8\}$ with the operation of multiplication modulo 9 forms a group G.

(a) By considering the closure of G, find the integers p and q where $0 < p < q < 9$.

(b) State the inverse of each element of G, and write down all the subgroups of G.

(c) Given that $\omega = \cos\frac{1}{3}\pi + i\sin\frac{1}{3}\pi$, and H is the group $\{\omega,\omega^2,\omega^3,\omega^4,\omega^5,\omega^6\}$ under multiplication of complex numbers, find with reasons whether G and H are isomorphic.

(OCR)

5 (a) Prove that the set $\{1,3,5,9,11,13\}$ together with the operation of multiplication modulo 14 forms a group G. (You may assume that the operation is associative.)

List all the subgroups of G with fewer than three elements.

(b) The group of symmetry transformations of the equilateral triangle under the operation of composition is H. Describe geometrically the six elements of H.

(c) Determine, with reasons, whether G and H are isomorphic.

Find a subgroup of G with three elements. Is it isomorphic to a subgroup of H? (OCR)

6 Prove that the set $\{1,2,4,7,8,k,13,14\}$ together with the operation multiplication modulo 15 forms a group G, provided k takes one particular value. State this value of k. (You may assume that the operation is associative, but the other axioms for a group must be clearly verified.)

If H is a subgroup of G of order n, use Lagrange's theorem to find all the possible values of n.

Find three subgroups of order 4, each containing the elements 1 and 4, and prove that exactly two of them are isomorphic. (OCR)

7 Given that the multiplication of complex numbers is associative, show that the set $\{1,-1,i,-i\}$ forms a group G under multiplication of complex numbers.

Prove also that the set $\{1,7,18,24\}$ under multiplication modulo 25 forms a group H.

Determine, with reasons, whether G and H are isomorphic. (OCR)

8 (a) The law of composition $*$ is defined by $a*b = a+b-ab$. Given that a, b and c are real numbers, prove that $a*(b*c) = (a*b)*c$.

(b) The law of composition $\circ$ is defined by $a\circ b = a+b-ab$ evaluated modulo 7 so that $2\circ 4 = 5$ for example.

Copy and complete the combination table for the set $\{0,2,3,4,5,6\}$ with law of composition $\circ$.

$\circ$	0	2	3	4	5	6
0	0	2	3	4	5	6
2	2	0	6	5	4	3

(c) Prove that the set $\{0,2,3,4,5,6\}$ forms a group G under $\circ$.

(d) Determine, with reasons, whether G is isomorphic to the group of rotations of the regular hexagon. (OCR)

9 The elements of the group G_n are the number 1 and the integers between 1 and n which have no factor in common with n; for example, the elements of G_4 are 1, 3. The operation of the group is multiplication modulo n. Write out the tables of G_5, G_8, G_{10} and G_{12}.

State which groups are isomorphic, giving your reasons. (OCR)

8 The algebra of sets

In Chapter 1 you learnt to use set language and found how to prove that two sets are equal. This chapter develops an algebra which enables you to simplify expressions involving sets and gives you another method for proving that sets are equal. When you have completed it, you should

- know, be able to prove and use the rules of set algebra
- know and be able to use De Morgan's laws
- know the definition of symmetric difference.

8.1 Strategy

In Example 1.6.1 you saw a proof that for any sets A and B, $A \cap B = B \cap A$. This proof enabled you to use $A \cap B = B \cap A$ to simplify expressions involving sets.

Also in Exercise 1C Question 5, if you tackled it, you proved that $A \cup B = B \cup A$.

$A \cap B = B \cap A$ and $A \cup B = B \cup A$ are the commutative rules for intersection and union.

Similarly, $(A \cap B) \cap C = A \cap (B \cap C)$ and $(A \cup B) \cup C = A \cup (B \cup C)$. These are the associative rules for intersection and union.

In this chapter, a number of similar rules are developed, and you will learn how to use them to simplify expressions involving sets and to prove that sets are equal.

8.2 Complementation

In Section 1.5 you met the idea of the complement of a set A. Fig. 8.1 shows the sets A and A', and the universal set U.

From Fig. 8.1 it looks as though $A \cup A' = U$ and $A \cap A' = \varnothing$. Example 8.2.1 proves the first of these relations.

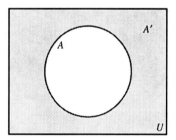

Fig. 8.1

Example 8.2.1
Prove that $A \cup A' = U$.

Proof
Remember, that to prove two sets are equal, you need to prove that each is a subset of the other, that is $A \cup A' \subseteq U$ and $U \subseteq A \cup A'$.

Proof of $A \cup A' \subseteq U$
All sets are a subset of U (definition of U), so $A \cup A' \subseteq U$.

Proof of $U \subseteq A \cup A'$
Suppose $x \in U$.

$$x \in U \implies x \in A \text{ or } x \in A' \qquad \text{(definition of } A')$$
$$\implies x \in A \cup A'.$$

Thus $U \subseteq A \cup A'$.

As $A \cup A' \subseteq U$ and $U \subseteq A \cup A'$, it follows that $A \cup A' = U$.

The proof of the result $A \cap A' = \emptyset$ is left to you in Exercise 8A Question 5.

The rules $A \cup A' = U$ and $A \cap A' = \emptyset$ are called the **complementation rules**.

Finally in this section, what can you say about the complement of a complement? Looking back at Fig. 8.1, the set of elements not in A', are in A. But remember, Venn diagrams do not constitute proof.

Example 8.2.2
Prove that $(A')' = A$.

Proof of $(A')' \subseteq A$
Suppose that $x \in (A')'$.

For the moment let $B = A'$. Then $x \in (A')'$ is the same as $x \in B'$, so $x \notin B$.

Using $B = A'$, this is $x \notin A'$, so $x \in A$.

Therefore, $(A')' \subseteq A$.

Proof of $A \subseteq (A')'$
Suppose that $x \in A$. Then $x \notin A'$.

For the moment let $B = A'$. Then $x \notin A'$ is the same as $x \notin B$, so $x \in B'$.

Using $B = A'$, $x \in B'$ is the same as $x \in (A')'$.

So, $A \subseteq (A')'$.

As $(A')' \subseteq A$ and $A \subseteq (A')'$, it follows that $(A')' = A$.

The rule $(A')' = A$ is called the **complement of a complement rule**.

8.3 The distributive rules

The commutative and associative rules for sets are very like those of addition and multiplication in arithmetic. Is there an equivalent set rule for the arithmetic rule $a \times (b + c) = (a \times b) + (a \times c)$, that is, the distributive rule?

Have a look at the Venn diagrams in Fig. 8.2.

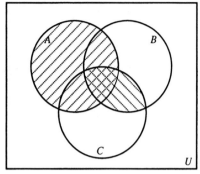
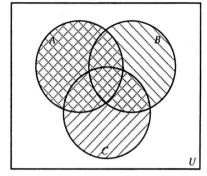

The region with any shading is $A \cup (B \cap C)$ The cross-shaded region is $(A \cup B) \cap (A \cup C)$

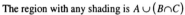
Fig. 8.2

From the diagram it certainly looks as though $A \cup (B \cap C) = (A \cup B) \cap (A \cup C)$.

Example 8.3.1 proves that this is true.

Example 8.3.1*
Prove that $A \cup (B \cap C) = (A \cup B) \cap (A \cup C)$.

Proof
There are two parts: the second part is left for you to prove in Exercise 8A Question 4.

Proof of $A \cup (B \cap C) \subseteq (A \cup B) \cap (A \cup C)$
Suppose $x \in A \cup (B \cap C)$.

$$x \in A \cup (B \cap C) \quad \Rightarrow \quad x \in A \text{ or } x \in B \cap C.$$

So there are two possibilities: either $x \in A$, or $x \in B \cap C$.

Taking the first of these,

$$x \in A \quad \Rightarrow \quad x \in A \cup B \text{ and } x \in A \cup C$$
$$\Rightarrow \quad x \in (A \cup B) \cap (A \cup C).$$

The other possibility, $x \in B \cap C$, gives

$$x \in B \cap C \quad \Rightarrow \quad x \in B \text{ and } x \in C$$
$$\Rightarrow \quad x \in A \cup B \text{ and } x \in A \cup C$$
$$\Rightarrow \quad x \in (A \cup B) \cap (A \cup C).$$

So either way, $x \in (A \cup B) \cap (A \cup C)$.

Hence $A \cup (B \cap C) \subseteq (A \cup B) \cap (A \cup C)$.

Proof of $(A \cup B) \cap (A \cup C) \subseteq A \cup (B \cap C)$
See Exercise 8A Question 4.

As $A \cup (B \cap C) \subseteq (A \cup B) \cap (A \cup C)$ and $(A \cup B) \cap (A \cup C) \subseteq A \cup (B \cap C)$, it follows that

$$A \cup (B \cap C) = (A \cup B) \cap (A \cup C).$$

$A \cup (B \cap C) = (A \cup B) \cap (A \cup C)$ is called the **distributive rule for union over intersection**.

However, it is also true that intersection is distributive over union.

So $A \cap (B \cup C) = (A \cap B) \cup (A \cap C)$. This is called the **distributive rule for intersection over union**.

8.4   Using the rules for the algebra of sets

You met the tautology and absorption rules in Example 1.6.3 and Exercise 1C Questions 7 and 8.

The tautology rules are $A \cap A = A$ and $A \cup A = A$,

and the absorption rules are $A \cap (A \cup B) = A$ and $A \cup (A \cap B) = A$.

Here is a summary of the rules proved (or established through an exercise) so far.

> Given any sets, A, B, C, and the universal set U then the following are true.
>
> The complementation rules
>
> $A \cap A' = \varnothing$ $A \cup A' = U$
>
> Complement of complement rule
>
> $(A')' = A$
>
> The commutative rules
>
> $A \cap B = B \cap A$ $A \cup B = B \cup A$
>
> The associative rules
>
> $(A \cap B) \cap C = A \cap (B \cap C)$ $(A \cup B) \cup C = A \cup (B \cup C)$
>
> The distributive rules
>
> $A \cup (B \cap C) = (A \cup B) \cap (A \cup C)$ $A \cap (B \cup C) = (A \cap B) \cup (A \cap C)$
>
> The tautology rules
>
> $A \cap A = A$ $A \cup A = A$
>
> The absorption rules
>
> $A \cap (A \cup B) = A$ $A \cup (A \cap B) = A$
>
> Rules involving $\varnothing$ and U
>
> $A \cap \varnothing = \varnothing$ $A \cup \varnothing = A$
>
> $A \cap U = A$ $A \cup U = U$
>
> $\varnothing' = U$ $U' = \varnothing$

The examples in the remainder of this section show how these rules can be used to simplify expressions involving sets.

Example 8.4.1

Simplify $\varnothing \cap A$.

$$\varnothing \cap A = A \cap \varnothing \qquad \text{(commutative rule)}$$
$$= \varnothing. \qquad \text{(rule involving } \varnothing)$$

Example 8.4.2

Prove that $(B \cup A') \cap B = B$.

$$(B \cup A') \cap B = B \cap (B \cup A') \qquad \text{(commutative rule)}$$
$$= (B \cap B) \cup (B \cap A') \qquad \text{(distributive rule)}$$
$$= B. \qquad \text{(absorption rule)}$$

Example 8.4.3

Simplify $A \cup (A' \cap B)$.

$$A \cup (A' \cap B) = (A \cup A') \cap (A \cup B) \qquad \text{(distributive rule)}$$
$$= U \cap (A \cup B) \qquad \text{(complementation rule)}$$
$$= A \cup B. \qquad \text{(rule involving } U)$$

Example 8.4.4

Simplify $(A \cup B) \cap (A' \cup B) \cap (A \cup B') \cap (A' \cup B')$.

$$(A \cup B) \cap (A \cup B') \cap (A' \cup B) \cap (A' \cup B')$$
$$= (A \cap (B \cup B')) \cap (A' \cup B) \cap (A' \cup B') \qquad \text{(distributive rule)}$$
$$= (A \cap U) \cap (A' \cup B) \cap (A' \cup B') \qquad \text{(complementation rule)}$$
$$= A \cap (A' \cup B) \cap (A' \cup B') \qquad \text{(rule involving } U)$$
$$= A \cap (A' \cup (B \cap B')) \qquad \text{(distributive rule)}$$
$$= A \cap (A' \cup \varnothing) \qquad \text{(complementation rule)}$$
$$= A \cap A' \qquad \text{(rule involving } \varnothing)$$
$$= \varnothing. \qquad \text{(complementation rule)}$$

Example 8.4.5

Simplify $(A' \cap (A \cup B')) \cup (B' \cap (B' \cup C)) \cup B'$.

$$(A' \cap (A \cup B')) \cup (B' \cap (B' \cup C)) \cup B'$$
$$= (A' \cap A) \cup (A' \cap B') \cup (B' \cap (B' \cup C)) \cup B' \qquad \text{(distributive rule)}$$
$$= \varnothing \cup (A' \cap B') \cup (B' \cap (B' \cup C)) \cup B' \qquad \text{(complementation rule)}$$
$$= (A' \cap B') \cup (B' \cap (B' \cup C)) \cup B' \qquad \text{(rule involving } \varnothing)$$
$$= (A' \cap B') \cup B' \cup B' \qquad \text{(absorption rule)}$$
$$= (A' \cap B') \cup B' \qquad \text{(tautology rule)}$$
$$= B'. \qquad \text{(absorption rule).}$$

Exercise 8A

1 Simplify the following.

(a) $\varnothing \cup A$ (b) $U \cap B$ (c) $U \cup B'$ (d) $A \cap (A \cup \varnothing)$

2 Prove that the following equations are correct.

(a) $(A \cup B') \cap B' = B'$

(b) $(A' \cup B') \cap (A \cup B) = (A \cap B') \cup (A' \cap B)$

(c) $A \cap (A' \cup B) \cap (A \cup B') = A \cap B$

3 Simplify each of the following expressions down to a single letter or symbol.

(a) $A' \cap B' \cap A$ (b) $B \cup (A \cup A')$

(c) $A' \cup B' \cup A' \cup B$ (d) $(A' \cup C) \cap (A' \cup B' \cup C') \cap (A' \cup C')$

4* Prove that $(A \cup B) \cap (A \cup C) \subseteq A \cup (B \cap C)$.

5 Prove that $A \cap A' = \varnothing$.

8.5 De Morgan's laws

De Morgan's laws are about simplifying $(A \cap B)'$ and $(A \cup B)'$. For example, how can you write them in terms of A, A', B and B'?

The Englishman Augustus De Morgan lived from 1806 to 1871.

Using Venn diagrams can help. See Fig. 8.3.

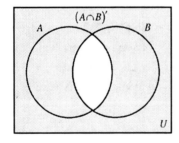
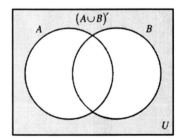

Fig. 8.3

The left diagram represents $(A \cap B)'$ and the right $(A \cup B)'$. The diagrams suggest that

$$(A \cap B)' = A' \cup B' \quad \text{and} \quad (A \cup B)' = A' \cap B'.$$

Theorem 8.1 shows how to prove the first of these. The second is left for you to prove Exercise 8B Question 5.

Theorem 8.1 (De Morgan's law)* $(A \cap B)' = A' \cup B'$

     Proof of $(A \cap B)' \subseteq A' \cup B'$
     Suppose that $x \in (A \cap B)'$. Then

$$x \in (A \cap B)' \quad \Rightarrow \quad x \notin (A \cap B)$$
$$\Rightarrow \quad x \in A' \text{ or } x \in B'$$
$$\Rightarrow \quad x \in (A' \cup B').$$

Thus $(A \cap B)' \subseteq A' \cup B'$.

Proof of $A' \cup B' \subseteq (A \cap B)'$
Suppose that $x \in A' \cup B'$.

$$x \in A' \cup B' \quad \Rightarrow \quad x \in A' \text{ or } x \in B'.$$

If $x \in A'$, then $x \notin A$, so $x \notin (A \cap B)$, showing $x \in (A \cap B)'$.

Similarly, if $x \in B'$, then $x \notin B$, so $x \notin A \cap B$, showing $x \in (A \cap B)'$.

Either way, $x \in (A \cap B)'$, so $A' \cup B' \subseteq (A \cap B)'$.

As $(A \cap B)' \subseteq A' \cup B'$ and $A' \cup B' \subseteq (A \cap B)'$, it follows that $(A \cap B)' = A' \cup B'$.

This is one of De Morgan's laws. The other is $(A \cup B)' = A' \cap B'$. They should be added to the list in Section 8.4.

> **De Morgan's laws**   If A and B are two subsets of a universal set,
>
> $$(A \cap B)' = A' \cup B' \quad \text{and} \quad (A \cup B)' = A' \cap B'.$$

De Morgan's laws give you another method for proving that sets are equal without needing to go back to first principles.

Example 8.5.1
Prove that if A and B are two subsets of a universal set, U, then
(a) $(A \cap B')' = A' \cup B$,   (b) $A \cap (A \cup B)' = \varnothing$.

(a) Using De Morgan's law $(A \cap B)' = A' \cup B'$ with B' in place of B gives

$$(A \cap B')' = A' \cup (B')' \qquad \text{(De Morgan's law)}$$
$$= A' \cup B. \qquad \text{(complement of complement rule)}$$

(b) Using De Morgan's second law on $(A \cup B)'$ and starting with the left side gives

$$A \cap (A \cup B)' = A \cap (A' \cap B') \qquad \text{(De Morgan's law)}$$
$$= (A \cap A') \cap B' \qquad \text{(associative rule)}$$
$$= \varnothing \cap B' \qquad \text{(complementation rule)}$$
$$= \varnothing. \qquad \text{(rule involving } \varnothing\text{)}$$

8.6   Set difference and symmetric difference

In Section 1.5 you were introduced to set difference, which was defined to be those elements of A which were not in B. That is, set difference $A \setminus B$ is defined by $A \setminus B = A \cap B'$. This is illustrated in Fig. 8.4.

Another operation on two sets, closely related to the set difference, is the **symmetric difference**. This is illustrated in Fig. 8.5.

The shaded region is the symmetric difference of A and B. It is denoted by $A \triangle B$ and defined by

$$A \triangle B = (A \setminus B) \cup (B \setminus A).$$

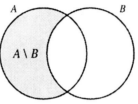

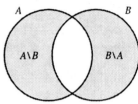

Fig. 8.4   Fig. 8.5

Let A and B be sets.

Then the set $A \triangle B = (A \setminus B) \cup (B \setminus A)$ is called the **symmetric difference** of A and B and is denoted by $A \triangle B$.

Alternatively, by substituting $A \cap B'$ and $A' \cap B$ for $A \setminus B$ and $B \setminus A$ respectively,

$$A \triangle B = (A \cap B') \cup (A' \cap B).$$

Example 8.6.1
Simplify $A \triangle \varnothing$.

$$\begin{aligned}
A \triangle \varnothing &= (A \cap \varnothing') \cup (A' \cap \varnothing) && \text{(using the alternative form)} \\
&= (A \cap U) \cup (A' \cap \varnothing) && \text{(rules involving } \varnothing \text{ and } U) \\
&= A \cup (A' \cap \varnothing) && \text{(rule involving } U) \\
&= A \cup \varnothing && \text{(rule involving } \varnothing) \\
&= A. && \text{(rule involving } \varnothing)
\end{aligned}$$

Example 8.6.2
Prove that $(A \setminus B) \cup (B \setminus A) = (A \cup B) \cap (A \cap B)'$.

$$\begin{aligned}
(A \setminus B) & \cup (B \setminus A) \\
&= (A \cap B') \cup (A' \cap B) && \text{(alternative form)} \\
&= ((A \cap B') \cup A') \cap ((A \cap B') \cup B) && \text{(distributive rule)} \\
&= (A' \cup (A \cap B')) \cap (B \cup (A \cap B')) && \text{(commutative rule } (\times 2)) \\
&= ((A' \cup A) \cap (A' \cup B')) \cap ((B \cup A) \cap (B \cup B')) && \text{(distributive rule } (\times 2)) \\
&= (U \cap (A' \cup B')) \cap ((B \cup A) \cap U) && \text{(complementation rule } (\times 2)) \\
&= (A' \cup B') \cap (B \cup A) && \text{(rule involving } U \; (\times 2)) \\
&= (A \cup B) \cap (A' \cup B') && \text{(commutative rule } (\times 2)) \\
&= (A \cup B) \cap (A \cap B)'. && \text{(De Morgan's law)}
\end{aligned}$$

Exercise 8B

1 Simplify the following.

   (a) $\left(A' \cup B\right)'$ (b) $\left(A' \cap B'\right)'$

2 Simplify the following.

   (a) $A \, \Delta \, A$ (b) $A \, \Delta \, \varnothing$ (c) $A \, \Delta \, U$

   (d) $B \cup (A \setminus B)$ (e) $A \setminus (A \setminus B)$ (f) $A \, \Delta \, (A \setminus B)$

3 Prove that if A, B and C are three sets, and if $A \cap B = A \cap C$ and $A \cup B = A \cup C$, then $B = C$. (Hint: start with $B = B \cap (A \cup B)$ and use $A \cup B = A \cup C$.)

4 Prove that $B \cap (A \setminus B) = \varnothing$.

5* Prove that $\left(A \cup B\right)' = A' \cap B'$.

6 Let $A = \{1, 2, 3, 4\}$ and $B = \{3, 4, 5, 6\}$. List the elements of

   (a) $A \, \Delta \, B$,   (b) $A \setminus B$,   (c) $B \setminus A$,   (d) $(A \, \Delta \, B) \setminus B$.

7 Draw a Venn diagram to illustrate $A \, \Delta \, (B \, \Delta \, C)$. Explain why the result suggests that $A \, \Delta \, (B \, \Delta \, C) = (A \, \Delta \, B) \, \Delta \, C$.

   Prove the result algebraically.

8 Simplify the following expressions.

   (a) $\left(A \cap B'\right)' \cup A'$ (b) $\left(A' \cap B\right)' \cup A'$

9 Prove that $\left((A \cap C) \cup (B \cap C')\right)' = (A' \cap C) \cup (B' \cap C')$.

10 Prove that $(A \setminus B) \setminus C = (A \setminus C) \setminus (B \setminus C)$.

Review exercise

1 Let G be a commutative group. Prove that the set of elements of order 2 together with the identity element, that is $H = \{a \in G : a^2 = e\}$, is a subgroup of G.

2 G is a commutative group, and $H = \{x \in G : x^3 = e\}$. Prove that H is a subgroup of G.

3 The binary operation $*$ on $\mathbb{R} \times \mathbb{R}$ is defined by $(a,b)*(c,d) = (ac - bd, ac + bd)$.

(a) Prove that $*$ is closed.

(b) What would you need to do to prove that $*$ is associative? (You do not need to prove this.)

(c) Assuming that $*$ is associative, prove that $\mathbb{R} \times \mathbb{R}$ with the operation $*$ is a group, and write down its identity element.

4 (a) Sketch the graph of the function f defined by $f : \mathbb{R} \to \mathbb{R}$ where $f(x) = e^{-x^2}$, and state its range.

(b) Determine whether f is injective and whether f is surjective, and justify your answers.

(c) A new function g is to be defined such that $g : A \to B$, where $A \subseteq \mathbb{R}$ and $B \subseteq \mathbb{R}$ such that $g(x) = e^{-x^2}$ has an inverse. Give examples of suitable sets A and B.

5 The relation R is defined on $\mathbb{C}$ by $(a + bi)R(c + di) \iff a^2 + b^2 = c^2 + d^2$, where $a, b, c, d \in \mathbb{R}$. Investigate whether or not R is an equivalence relation: if R is not an equivalence relation, say why; if R is an equivalence relation, find its equivalence classes.

6 In S_4, the permutations a and b are given by $a = \begin{pmatrix} 1 & 2 & 3 & 4 \\ 2 & 4 & 1 & 3 \end{pmatrix}$ and $b = \begin{pmatrix} 1 & 2 & 3 & 4 \\ 1 & 4 & 3 & 2 \end{pmatrix}$.

(a) Using a similar notation, calculate the permutations a^2, a^{-1}, ab and ab^{-1}.

(b) Calculate the orders of a and b.

7 You are given that the set $\{1,2,3,\ldots,12\}$ forms a group G under multiplication modulo 13. A subgroup with n elements is said to have order n. Find, or explain why none exists, a subgroup of G with order

(a) 2,   (b) 3,   (c) 5.   (OCR)

8 The set $\{a,b,c,d\}$ under the binary operation $*$ forms a group G of order 4 with the following operation table.

$*$	a	b	c	d
a	d	a	b	c
b	a	b	c	d
c	b	c	d	a
d	c	d	a	b

(a) Find the order of each element of G.

(b) Write down a proper subgroup of G.   (OCR)

9 The functions $i(x)$, $a(x)$, $b(x)$, $c(x)$ are defined for all $x \neq 0$, $x \neq 1$ by

$$i(x) = x, \quad a(x) = \frac{1}{x}, \quad b(x) = 1 - x \quad \text{and} \quad c(x) = \frac{1}{1-x}.$$

The operation $\otimes$ is defined as the composition of functions: that is,

$$(p \otimes q)(x) = pq(x) = p\{q(x)\}.$$

(a) Show that the set of functions $\{i, a, b, c\}$ is not closed under $\otimes$, and find two further functions $d(x)$ and $e(x)$ such that $\{i, a, b, c, d, e\}$ is closed under $\otimes$.

(b) Copy and complete the composition table for the set $G = \{i, a, b, c, d, e\}$, under $\otimes$.

$\otimes$	i	a	b	c	d	e
i	i	a	b	c	d	e
a	a	i		b		
b	b		i			
c	c		a		i	
d	d			i		a
e	e	c			i	

(c) Hence show that $(G, \otimes)$ forms a group. (You may assume that the composition of functions is associative.)

(d) Find whether G is a commutative group, giving reasons.

(e) Find whether G is a cyclic group, giving reasons.

(f) Write down all the subgroups of G. (OCR)

10 Show that the matrices $\begin{pmatrix} a & b \\ c & d \end{pmatrix}$, where $ad \neq bc$, form a group G under matrix multiplication. Show that the following subsets of G form subgroups of G.

(a) $\begin{pmatrix} a & b \\ 0 & 1 \end{pmatrix}$　　　　(b) $\begin{pmatrix} 1 & b \\ 0 & 1 \end{pmatrix}$　　　　(c) $\begin{pmatrix} a & 0 \\ 0 & 1 \end{pmatrix} (a \neq 0)$

(d) Find a proper subgroup of (a) which contains (b) as a proper subgroup.

(e) Find a subgroup of G of order 4.

11 (a) The elements a, b and c are elements of a non-commutative group G. Prove that $(abc)^{-1} = c^{-1}b^{-1}a^{-1}$.

(b) A group H contains distinct elements x, y and e, where e is the identity element. Given that $xy = y^2x$, prove that $xy \neq yx$. (OCR)

12 The law of composition $*$ is defined by $a * b = a + b - 2$ where a and b are numbers in arithmetic modulo 6.

(a) Show that the set $\{0, 1, 2, 3, 4, 5\}$ forms a group G under $*$ in arithmetic modulo 6.

(b) Find all the subgroups of G.

13 Let $S = \{1,2,3,4\}$ and f be a function whose domain and range are both S, defined by

$f(x)$ = the remainder when $2x$ is divided by 5.

(a) Prove that f is a bijection.   (b) Show that the composite function $f \circ f$ is the identity.

14 The set S consists of the eight elements 9^1, 9^2, ... , 9^8 where the operation is multiplication modulo 64. Determine each of the elements of S as an integer between 0 and 63.

Under multiplication modulo 64, the set S forms a group G with identity 1. Write down the inverses of each of the remaining elements of G.

A group in which each element x can be written as a power of a particular element g of the group is said to be a cyclic group; and such an element g is called a generator of the group. Write down all the possible generators of G.

15 Construct the composition table for $(S, \circ)$, where the binary operation $\circ$ is defined on the set $S = \{0,1,2,3,4,5,6\}$ by $x \circ y = x + y - xy$ modulo 7.

One of the elements of S is removed to form a set S' of order 6, such that $(S', \circ)$ forms a group. State which element is to be deleted, and prove that $(S', \circ)$ is a group.

16 Let A and B be sets. Show that A and B with the operation of symmetric difference generate a group (G, Δ). (You may assume that sets are associative under the operation Δ.)

Write down the order of each element of G.

17 Let G be a group and H be a subgroup of G. The relation R is defined on the elements of G by $aRb \iff ab^{-1} \in H$. Prove that R is an equivalence relation, and find the equivalence classes.

18 Let H and K be finite subgroups of a finite group G, and let the orders of H and K be relatively prime; that is, they have no common factors apart from 1. Prove that the only element common to H and K is the identity element.

Examination questions

1 (a) The difference, $A - B$, of two sets A and B is defined as the set of all elements of A which do not belong to B.

(i)   Show by means of a Venn diagram that $A - B = A \cap B'$.

(ii)   Using set algebra, prove that $A - (B \cup C) = (A - B) \cap (A - C)$.

(b) Let S be the set of all 2×2 non-singular matrices each of whose elements is either 0 or 1. Two matrices belonging to S are $\begin{pmatrix} 0 & 1 \\ 1 & 0 \end{pmatrix}$ and $\begin{pmatrix} 1 & 1 \\ 0 & 1 \end{pmatrix}$.

Write down the other four members of S.

(c) You are given that S forms a group under matrix multiplication, when the elements of the matrix product are calculated modulo 2.

(i)   Find the order of all the members of S whose determinant is negative.

(ii)   Hence find a subgroup of S of order 3.

(d) The group $(G, *)$ is defined on the set $\{e,a,b,c\}$, where e denotes the identity element. Prove that $a * b = b * a$.

(© IBO 2004)

2 (a) Let A, B and C be subsets of a given universal set.

   (i)   Use a Venn diagram to show that $(A \cap B) \cup C = (A \cup C) \cap (B \cup C)$.

   (ii) Hence, and by using De Morgan's laws, show that $(A' \cap B) \cup C' = (A \cap C)' \cap (B' \cap C)'$.

(b) Let R be a relation on $\mathbb{Z}$ such that for $m \in \mathbb{Z}^+$, xRy if and only if m divides $x - y$, where $x, y \in \mathbb{Z}$.

   (i)   Prove that R is an equivalence relation on $\mathbb{Z}$.

   (ii) Prove that this equivalence relation partitions $\mathbb{Z}$ into m distinct classes.

   (iii) Let $\mathbb{Z}_m$ be the set of all the equivalence classes found in part (b). Define a suitable binary operation $+_m$ on $\mathbb{Z}_m$ and prove that $(\mathbb{Z}_m, +_m)$ is an additive Abelian group.

   (iv) Let $(K, \Diamond)$ be a cyclic group of order m. Prove that $(K, \Diamond)$ is isomorphic to $\mathbb{Z}_m$.

(c) Let $(G, \circ)$ be a group with subgroups $(H, \circ)$ and $(K, \circ)$. Prove that $(H \cup K, \circ)$ is a subgroup of $(G, \circ)$ if and only if one of the sets H and K is contained in the other.   (© IBO 2002)

3 The operation $\#$ defined on the set $\{a,b,c,d,e\}$ has the following operation table.

#	a	b	c	d	e
a	d	c	e	a	b
b	e	d	a	b	c
c	b	e	d	c	a
d	a	b	c	d	e
e	c	a	b	e	d

(a) Show that only three of the four group axioms are satisfied.

Let R be a relation defined on 2×2 matrices such that, given the matrices A and B, ARB if and only if there exists a matrix H such that $A = HBH^{-1}$.

(b) Show that R is an equivalence relation.

(c) Show that all matrices in the same equivalence class have equal determinants.

(d) Given the matrix $M = \begin{pmatrix} 1 & 2 \\ 1 & 3 \end{pmatrix}$, find a 2×2 matrix that is

   (i)   related to M (excluding M itself),

   (ii) not related to M.

(e) Let $(G, *)$ be a group, and H a subset of G. Given that for all $a, b \in H$, $a^{-1}b \in H$, prove that $(H, *)$ is a subgroup of $(G, *)$.   (© IBO 2005)

4 Let $S = \{2,4,6,8,10,12,14\}$. The relation R is defined on S such that for $a, b \in S$, aRb if and only if $a^2 = b^2 (\text{modulo } 6)$.

(a) Show that R is an equivalence relation.

(b) Find all the equivalence classes.   (© IBO 2006)

5   The function f is defined by $f : \mathbb{R} \to \mathbb{R}$ where $f(x) = e^{\sin x} - 1$.

(a) Find the exact range, A, of f.

(b) (i)   Explain why f is not an injection.

(ii)   Giving a reason, state whether or not f is a surjection.

(c) The function g is now defined to be $g : [-k, k] \to A$, where $g(x) = e^{\sin x} - 1$ and $k > 0$.

(i)   Find the maximum value of k for which g is an injection.

For this value of k,

(ii)   find an expression for $g^{-1}(x)$,

(iii) write down the domain of g^{-1}.   (© IBO 2006)

Answers

1 The language of sets

Exercise 1A (page 3)

1. (a) $A = \{1, 2, 4, 8, 16, 32\}$
   (b) $B = \{1, 2, 3, 4, 5, 6\}$
   (c) $C = \varnothing$
   (d) $D = \{\sqrt{2}\}$
   (e) $E = \{-\sqrt{2}, \sqrt{2}\}$
   (f) $F = \{0, \pm 1, \pm 2, \dots\} = \mathbb{Z}$
   (g) $G = \{0, \pm 2, \pm 4, \dots\}$
   (h) $H = \{4, 5, 6, 7\}$
   Sets F and G are infinite; all the others are finite.

2. (a) Well-defined
   (b) This may be well-defined in a particular country, but given different time zones, and the difficulty of determining the exact time of birth, it is probably better avoided.
   (c) Well-defined. Note that it may be very difficult to find out what it is.

3. $2\mathbb{Z} = \{0, \pm 2, \pm 4, \dots\}$, $\{\pm 1, \pm 3, \pm 5, \dots\}$

Exercise 1B (page 8)

1. (a) $\{1, 2, 4, 6, 8\}$ (b) $\{2\}$
   (c) $\{0, 3, 4, 6, 7, 8\}$ (d) $\{4, 8\}$
   (e) $\{4, 6, 8\}$ (f) $\{0, 1, 3, 4, 5, 6, 7, 8\}$
   (g) $\{0, 3, 6, 7\}$ (h) $\{4, 6, 8\}$

2. (a) E (b) I (c) $\varnothing$
   (d) Isosceles triangles, but not equilateral ones
   (e) E (f) R (g) $\varnothing$
   (h) Non-isosceles right-angled triangles

3. (a) S (b) S (c) D (d) R

Exercise 1C (page 12)

1. $P \subseteq Q$

2. $P \subseteq Q$

3. (a) $\varnothing$ (b) A (c) A
   (d) U (e) U (f) $\varnothing$

4. A

10. U

Exercise 1D (page 14)

1. (a) $\{(H,1),(H,2),(H,3),(H,4),(H,5),(H,6),$ $(T,1),(T,2),(T,3),(T,4),(T,5),(T,6)\}$

(b) $\{(1,H),(1,T),(2,H),(2,T),(3,H),(3,T),$ $(4,H),(4,T),(5,H),(5,T),(6,H),(6,T)\}$

2. (a) False (b) False

3. $A \times B \times C = \{(a,b,c) \mid a \in A, b \in B, c \in C\}$
   $(0,0,0),(0,0,1),(0,1,0),(1,0,0),(0,1,1),(1,0,1),$ $(1,1,0),(1,1,1)$

5. $\mathbb{Z} \times \mathbb{Z}$ is the set of points in the plane which have integer coordinates for both x and y.

2 Equivalence relations

Exercise 2A (page 16)

1. (a)
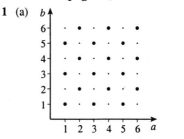
$\overline{1} = \overline{3} = \overline{5} = \{1, 3, 5\}$, $\overline{2} = \overline{4} = \overline{6} = \{2, 4, 6\}$

(b)
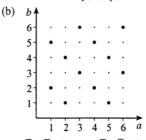
$\overline{1} = \overline{4} = \{2, 5\}$, $\overline{2} = \overline{5} = \{1, 4\}$,
$\overline{3} = \overline{6} = \{3, 6\}$

(c)
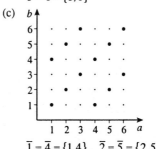
$\overline{1} = \overline{4} = \{1, 4\}$, $\overline{2} = \overline{5} = \{2, 5\}$,
$\overline{3} = \overline{6} = \{3, 6\}$

(d)

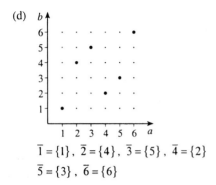

$\overline{1} = \{1\}$, $\overline{2} = \{4\}$, $\overline{3} = \{5\}$, $\overline{4} = \{2\}$
$\overline{5} = \{3\}$, $\overline{6} = \{6\}$

Exercise 2B (page 21)

1 The equivalence classes are
(a) lines passing through the origin, but not including the origin;
(b) equivalent fractions, that is, the elements of $\mathbb{Q}$;
(c) even integers and odd integers;
(d) integers which leave remainders 0, 1 and 2 when divided by 3;
(e) $\{\pm x \mid x \in \mathbb{Z}\}$.

2 (a) Not an equivalence relation, since $1R0$ but 0 is not related to 1, since -1 is not a perfect square.
(b) Not an equivalence relation, since 0 is not related to 0, as $0 \times 0 \not> 0$.
(c) This is an equivalence relation, as, trivially, all the conditions are satisfied. There is just one equivalence class, that of $\mathbb{Z}^+$ itself.
(d) Not an equivalence relation, since $1R0$ and $0R-1$, but 1 is not related to -1.
(e) Not an equivalence relation, since $0R\frac{1}{2}$ and $\frac{1}{2}R1$, but 0 is not related to 1.
(f) Not an equivalence relation, since $1R2$ and $2R3$, but 1 is not related to 3.
(g) This is an equivalence relation provided you agree that a line is parallel to itself. The equivalence classes are sets of parallel lines in the plane.
(h) Not an equivalence relation, since $(1,1)$ is not related to $(1,1)$.
(i) This is an equivalence relation if you agree that a triangle is similar to itself. The equivalence classes are sets of similar triangles.
(j) This is an equivalence relation. The solution is identical to that of part (i), with the word 'congruent' replacing 'similar'.
(k) Not an equivalence relation, since l is not perpendicular to itself.

3 The equivalence classes are lines in the plane $\mathbb{R}^2$ which are parallel to $y = x$.

4 The equivalence classes are squares with centres at the origin. The sides of the squares are parallel to the axes.

5 The equivalence classes are squares with centres at the origin. The vertices of the squares lie on the axes.

6 The equivalence classes are circles with centres at the origin.

3 Functions

Exercise 3A (page 28)

2 For example, $f:\mathbb{R} \to \mathbb{R}$, where $f(x) = e^x$
3 For example, $f:\mathbb{R} \to [-1,1]$, where $f(x) = \sin x$
4 (a) Function; not an injection; not a surjection
(b) Function; injection; surjection
(c) Not a function (undefined at 0)
(d) Function; not an injection; not a surjection
(e) Not a function (undefined at $\left(n+\frac{1}{2}\right)\pi$, $n \in \mathbb{Z}$)
(f) Function; injection; not a surjection
(g) Function; not an injection; not a surjection
(h) Not a function (undefined for $x \in \mathbb{R} \setminus \left(\mathbb{R}^+ \cup \{0\}\right)$)
(i) Function; injection; surjection
(j) Function; not an injection; not a surjection
(k) Not a function (undefined for $x \in \mathbb{R} \setminus [-1,1]$)
(l) Not a function (no such number exists)

8 (a) Every y-value of the function has at most one x-value corresponding to it.
(b) Every y-value of the function has at least one x-value corresponding to it.
(c) Every y-value of the function has exactly one x-value corresponding to it.

9 (a) False   (b) True   (c) True

10 (a) Function; not an injection; surjection
(b) Not a function; $f(p)$ is not uniquely specified
(c) Function; injection; not a surjection
(d) Function; injection; not a surjection

Exercise 3B (page 35)

2 (a) Not surjective
(b) Not injective
(c) Not bijective

3 The only bijections are (b) and (i).

(b) The inverse is $f^{-1}:\mathbb{R} \to \mathbb{R}$ where
$$f^{-1}(x) = x^{\frac{1}{3}}.$$

(i) The inverse is $f^{-1}:\mathbb{R} \to \mathbb{R}$ where
$$f^{-1}(x) = x - 1.$$

5 (a) False (b) True (c) True (d) True
(e) False (f) True (g) False

6 The equivalence classes are
$$\{x \mid x \in \mathbb{R}, f(x) = k, k \in \text{range } f\}.$$
$$\{\tfrac{1}{8}\pi + n\pi, \tfrac{3}{8}\pi + n\pi \mid n \in \mathbb{Z}\}$$

7 (b) $f^{-1}(x) = 2(x-1)$, $g^{-1}(x) = \ln x$
(c) $h^{-1}(x) = 2(\ln x - 1)$

8 $f^{-1}(x,y) = (4x - 2y, -5x + 3y)$

9 f is injective, surjective and bijective;
g is none of these.

10 (a) -1 (b) -1 (c) -1

4 Binary operations and groups

Exercise 4A (page 42)

1 (a) Binary operation: not closed;
not commutative; not associative
(b) Binary operation: closed;
not commutative; associative
(c) Binary operation: closed;
not commutative; not associative
(d) Binary operation: closed;
commutative; not associative
(e) Binary operation: closed;
commutative; associative
(f) Not a binary operation as B^{-1} does not exist
for all 2×2 matrices
(i) Binary operation: closed; commutative;
associative
(g) Binary operation: closed;
not commutative; associative
(h) Binary operation: closed;
not commutative; not associative
(i) Binary operation: closed;
commutative; associative
(j) Not a binary operation as there is no
smallest number greater than $a + b$

2 (a) True (b) True

3 (a) True (b) True

Exercise 4B (page 44)

1 $s \circ t = p$, $t \circ s = q$, $(p \circ q) \circ s = s$, $p \circ (q \circ t) = t$,
$r, s; q, p$

$s \circ t = q$, $t \circ s = p$, $(p \circ q) \circ s = r$, $p \circ (q \circ t) = t$,
$r, u; p, q$

2 (a) No identity
(b) Identity I; no general inverse
(c) Identity $1 + 0i$; no general inverse, e.g. 0
(d) No identity
(e) No identity

3 (a) Identity $\begin{pmatrix} 1 & 1 \\ 0 & 0 \end{pmatrix}$; inverse $\begin{pmatrix} x^{-1} & x^{-1} \\ 0 & 0 \end{pmatrix}$

(b) Identity 6; inverses of 2, 4, 6 and 8 are 8, 4,
6 and 2.
(c) Identity 0; inverses of 0, 2, 4, 6 and 8 are 0,
8, 6, 4 and 2.
(d) Identity 1; inverses of 1, 3, 7 and 9 are 1, 7,
3 and 9.

Exercise 4C (page 50)

1 (a) Not a group; no identity element.
(c) Not a group; 2 has no inverse.
(e) Not a group; not closed.
(g) Not a group; 5 has no inverse.
(i) Not a group; 0 has no inverse.
All the rest are groups.

2 There is no identity element.

3 $x \mapsto \dfrac{x-1}{x}$, $x \mapsto \dfrac{x}{x-1}$

6 If $a \circ b = e$, a and b would be inverse elements
of G and e, a and b would form a group with
three elements.
If $a \circ b = a$, then b would be the identity, a
contradiction. Similarly, if $a \circ b = b$, then a
would be the identity.

8 $x \mapsto a^{-1}(x - b)$

9 a^3

5 Some examples of groups

Exercise 5A (page 56)

1

	0	1	2	3	4
0	0	1	2	3	4
1	1	2	3	4	0
2	2	3	4	0	1
3	3	4	0	1	2
4	4	0	1	2	3

The inverse of 2 is 3. $x = 4$; $y = 3$

2	1	2	3	4	5	6
1	1	2	3	4	5	6
2	2	4	6	1	3	5
3	3	6	2	5	1	4
4	4	1	5	2	6	3
5	5	3	1	6	4	2
6	6	5	4	3	2	1

The inverse of 3 is 5, and the inverse of 4 is 2.

3	1	2	3	4	5
1	1	2	3	4	5
2	2	4		2	4
3	3		3		3
4	4	2		4	2
5	5	4	3	2	1

The operation is not closed as 2×3 is not in the set. If q is not prime, then $q = mn$ for some

$$q = m, n \in \left(\mathbb{Z}_q \setminus \{0\}, \times \right); \quad mn = q \notin \left(\mathbb{Z}_q \setminus \{0\}, \times \right),$$

so the operation is not closed.

4	1	2	4	7	8	11	13	14
1	1	2	4	7	8	11	13	14
2	2	4	8	14	1	7	11	13
4	4	8	1	13	2	14	7	11
7	7	14	13	4	11	2	1	8
8	8	1	2	11	4	13	14	7
11	11	7	14	2	13	1	8	4
13	13	11	7	1	14	8	4	2
14	14	13	11	8	7	4	2	1

11

5 9

6 4, 1;   (a) 15   (b) 17   (c) 19   (d) 53

7	0	1	2	3	4
0	2	3	4	0	1
1	3	4	0	1	2
2	4	0	1	2	3
3	0	1	2	3	4
4	1	2	3	4	0

The identity is 3, and the inverses of 0, 1, 2, 3 and 4 are 1, 0, 4, 3 and 2 respectively.

Exercise 5B (page 57)

1	I	X	Y	H
I	I	X	Y	H
X	X	I	H	Y
Y	Y	H	I	X
H	H	Y	X	I

2 S and X; for RAR^{-1} the elements are I, R, S, Y, X and Z and for XAX^{-1} they are I, S, R, X, Z and Y. $A = R$

3 D_4	I	R	R^2	R^3	H	L	V	M
I	I	R	R^2	R^3	H	L	V	M
R	R	R^2	R^3	I	M	H	L	V
R^2	R^2	R^3	I	R	V	M	H	L
R^3	R^3	I	R	R^2	L	V	M	H
H	H	L	V	M	I	R	R^2	R^3
L	L	V	M	H	R^3	I	R	R^2
V	V	M	H	L	R^2	R^3	I	R
M	M	H	L	V	R	R^2	R^3	I

4 R

Exercise 5C (page 62)

1 $ab = \begin{pmatrix} 1 & 2 & 3 & 4 & 5 \\ 3 & 4 & 1 & 2 & 5 \end{pmatrix}$

$ba = \begin{pmatrix} 1 & 2 & 3 & 4 & 5 \\ 1 & 4 & 5 & 2 & 3 \end{pmatrix}$

$a^2 b = \begin{pmatrix} 1 & 2 & 3 & 4 & 5 \\ 4 & 1 & 5 & 3 & 2 \end{pmatrix}$

$ac^{-1} = \begin{pmatrix} 1 & 2 & 3 & 4 & 5 \\ 2 & 4 & 3 & 1 & 5 \end{pmatrix}$

$(ac)^{-1} = \begin{pmatrix} 1 & 2 & 3 & 4 & 5 \\ 4 & 1 & 3 & 2 & 5 \end{pmatrix}$

$c^{-1} ac = \begin{pmatrix} 1 & 2 & 3 & 4 & 5 \\ 3 & 4 & 2 & 5 & 1 \end{pmatrix}$

2 $x = a^{-1} b = \begin{pmatrix} 1 & 2 & 3 & 4 & 5 \\ 5 & 2 & 3 & 1 & 4 \end{pmatrix}$

$x = a^{-1} cb^{-1} = \begin{pmatrix} 1 & 2 & 3 & 4 & 5 \\ 4 & 1 & 2 & 5 & 3 \end{pmatrix}$

3 (a) $\begin{pmatrix} 1 & 2 & 3 \\ 1 & 3 & 2 \end{pmatrix}$ (b) $\begin{pmatrix} 1 & 2 & 3 \\ 2 & 1 & 3 \end{pmatrix}$

(c) $\begin{pmatrix} 1 & 2 & 3 \\ 3 & 1 & 2 \end{pmatrix}$ (d) $\begin{pmatrix} 1 & 2 & 3 \\ 3 & 2 & 1 \end{pmatrix}$

(e) $\begin{pmatrix} 1 & 2 & 3 \\ 2 & 1 & 3 \end{pmatrix}$ (f) $\begin{pmatrix} 1 & 2 & 3 \\ 3 & 1 & 2 \end{pmatrix}$

(g) $\begin{pmatrix} 1 & 2 & 3 \\ 1 & 2 & 3 \end{pmatrix}$ (h) $\begin{pmatrix} 1 & 2 & 3 \\ 2 & 3 & 1 \end{pmatrix}$

6 Subgroups

Exercise 6A (page 67)

1 $5^1 = 5$, $5^2 = 7$, $5^3 = 8$, $5^4 = 4$, $5^5 = 2$, $5^6 = 1$; there are six distinct powers.

2 (a) 0, 1; 1, 6; 2, 3; 3, 2; 4, 3; 5, 6
   (b) 1, 1; 2, 10; 3, 6; 4, 5; 5, 5; 6, 10; 7, 10; 8, 10; 9, 5; 10, 2
   (c) I, 1; R, 4; R^2, 2; R^3, 4; H, 2; L, 2; V, 2; M, 2

3 X, Y, H

4 i, $-i$; 2

5 1, -1

6 For example, any matrix of the form $\begin{pmatrix} 1 & k \\ 0 & -1 \end{pmatrix}$ where $k \in \mathbb{N}$ has order 2.

7 Yes; 5 is a generator.

8 2 (and -2) are both generators.

9 The first is not cyclic, since $a^2 = b^2 = c^2 = e$; the second is cyclic, with a and c as generators.

10 1, 2, 3 and 4 are generators of $(\mathbb{Z}_5, +)$; 1 and 5 are generators of $(\mathbb{Z}_6, +)$.

Exercise 6B (page 72)

1 (a) I, 1; R, 4; R^2, 2; R^3, 4; H, 2; L, 2; V, 2; M, 2
   (b) $\{I\}$, $\{I, R^2\}$, $\{I, H\}$, $\{I, L\}$, $\{I, V\}$, $\{I, M\}$, $\{I, R, R^2, R^3\}$
   (c) $\{I, H, R^2, V\}$, $\{I, L, R^2, M\}$

2 (a) $(\{0\}, +)$, $(\{0,2\}, +)$, $(\mathbb{Z}_4, +)$
   (b) $(\{0\}, +)$, $(\mathbb{Z}_5, +)$

3 $\left\{\begin{pmatrix} 1 & 2 & 3 \\ 1 & 2 & 3 \end{pmatrix}, \begin{pmatrix} 1 & 2 & 3 \\ 3 & 1 & 2 \end{pmatrix}, \begin{pmatrix} 1 & 2 & 3 \\ 2 & 3 & 1 \end{pmatrix}\right\}$,

$\left\{\begin{pmatrix} 1 & 2 & 3 \\ 1 & 2 & 3 \end{pmatrix}, \begin{pmatrix} 1 & 2 & 3 \\ 1 & 3 & 2 \end{pmatrix}\right\}$,

$\left\{\begin{pmatrix} 1 & 2 & 3 \\ 1 & 2 & 3 \end{pmatrix}, \begin{pmatrix} 1 & 2 & 3 \\ 3 & 2 & 1 \end{pmatrix}\right\}$,

$\left\{\begin{pmatrix} 1 & 2 & 3 \\ 1 & 2 & 3 \end{pmatrix}, \begin{pmatrix} 1 & 2 & 3 \\ 2 & 1 & 3 \end{pmatrix}\right\}$

4 $\{1, -1\}$

8 (a) $\{I, R, S\}$ (b) $\{I, X\}$
   (c) $\left\{\begin{pmatrix} a & b \\ 0 & a \end{pmatrix} : a, b \in \mathbb{R}\right\}$ (d) $\{e, b, q, s\}$
   (e) $\{e, x, p\}$

9 $\{e\}$, $\{e, b\}$, $\{e, a, b, c\}$, $\{e, b, p, r\}$, $\{e, b, q, s\}$, Q_4

10 $\{e\}$, $\{e, a\}$, $\{e, b\}$, $\{e, c\}$, $\{e, x, p\}$, $\{e, y, q\}$, $\{e, z, r\}$, $\{e, t, s\}$, $\{e, a, b, c\}$, A_4

Exercise 6C (page 74)

1 1, 2, 3, 4, 6, 8, 12, 24

2 As 9 is not a factor of 15, Lagrange's theorem shows that a group of order 15 cannot have a subgroup of order 9.

3 1, p, q and pq

5 1, p and p^2; 1, p, p^2 and p^3

Exercise 6D (page 77)

1 $\{I, R, S\}$, $\{X, Y, Z\}$;
   $\{I\}$, $\{R\}$, $\{S\}$, $\{X\}$, $\{Y\}$, $\{Z\}$
   D_3

2 $\{0, 3\}$, $\{1, 4\}$, $\{2, 5\}$

3 (a) $\{e, a, b, c\}$, $\{x, y, z, t\}$, $\{p, q, r, s\}$
   (b) $\{e, x, p\}$, $\{a, t, r\}$, $\{b, y, s\}$, $\{c, z, q\}$

4 $\{0, \pm 3, \pm 6, \ldots\}$, $\{\ldots, -2, 1, 4, \ldots\}$, $\{\ldots, -1, 2, 5, \ldots\}$

7 Isomorphisms of groups

Exercise 7A (page 83)

3 2 is a generator of $(\mathbb{Z}_{13} \setminus \{0\}, \times (\mathrm{mod}\, 13))$. Define a function $f : \mathbb{Z}_{13} \to \mathbb{Z}_{12}$ by the rule $f(2^n) = n$ and show that it is an isomorphism.

Exercise 7B (page 87)

1 (a)

	2	4	6	8
2	4	8	2	6
4	8	6	4	2
6	2	4	6	8
8	6	2	8	4

(b) 6; $2^{-1} = 8$, $4^{-1} = 4$, $6^{-1} = 6$, $8^{-1} = 2$

(c) Both groups are cyclic with generators 2 and i respectively, so they are isomorphic.

2 (a) $e, 1$; $a, 2$; $b, 4$; $b^2, 2$; $b^3, 4$; $ab, 2$; $ab^2, 2$; $ab^3, 3$

(b) 5 subgroups; $\{e,a\}$, $\{e,ab\}$, $\{e,ab^2\}$, $\{e,b^2\}$ and $\{e,ab^3\}$ all have order 2.

(c) $\{e,b,b^2,b^3\}$ and $\{e,ab,b^2,ab^3\}$

(d) By Lagrange's theorem the order of a subgroup of a finite group divides the order of the group. As 6 does not divide 8, there is no subgroup of order 6.

(e) M is commutative and D is not, $ab \neq ba$.

3 (a) 9, 17, 25, 33, 41, 49, 57, 1
Orders are 1, 1; 9, 8; 17, 4; 25, 8; 33, 2; 41, 8; 49, 4; 57, 8.
The possible generators are 9, 25, 41, 57.
The subgroups are $\{1\}$, $\{1,33\}$, $\{1,17,33,49\}$, G.

(b) G contains a generator, so it is cyclic. Every element of H apart from the identity has order 2, so H is not cyclic. Therefore G and H are not isomorphic.

4 (a) $p = 4$, $q = 5$

(b) 1 and 8 are self-inverse; the other inverses occur in pairs, 2, 5 and 4, 7; $\{1\}$, $\{1,8\}$, $\{1,4,7\}$, G.

(c) The order of the element 2 of G is 6, so G is cyclic. $\omega \in H$ has order 6, so H is cyclic. Therefore G and H are isomorphic.

5 (a) $\{1\}$, $\{1,13\}$

(b) The elements are the rotations of $\frac{2}{3}\pi$, $\frac{4}{3}\pi$ and 0 about the centre of the triangle, plus reflections in the lines of symmetry.

$\{1,9,11\}$ is a subgroup of G which is isomorphic to the subgroup of rotations of H.

6 $k = 11$. The possible values of n are 1, 2, 4 and 8. $\{1,4,7,13\}$, $\{1,2,4,8\}$ and $\{1,4,11,14\}$. The orders of the elements in these groups are 1, 2, 4, 4, 1, 4, 2, 4 and 1, 2, 2, 2. The first two groups both have generators, and are therefore cyclic

and isomorphic. The third group does not have a generator, and is not isomorphic to the other two.

7 The orders of the elements $\{1,-1,i,-i\}$ are 1, 2, 4, 4. The orders of the elements $\{1,7,18,24\}$ are 1, 4, 4, 2. Both groups have generators, and are therefore both cyclic and isomorphic.

8 (b)

	0	2	3	4	5	6
0	0	2	3	4	5	6
2	2	0	6	5	4	3
3	3	6	4	2	0	5
4	4	5	2	6	3	0
5	5	4	0	3	6	2
6	6	3	5	0	2	4

(d) 3 is a generator for G, so G is a cyclic group. The group of rotations of the regular hexagon has an element (rotation of angle $\frac{1}{3}\pi$) of order 6 and is cyclic. Therefore the groups are isomorphic.

9

G_5	1	2	3	4
1	1	2	3	4
2	2	4	1	3
3	3	1	4	2
4	4	3	2	1

G_8	1	3	5	7
1	1	3	5	7
3	3	1	7	5
5	5	7	1	3
7	7	5	3	1

G_{10}	1	3	7	9
1	1	3	7	9
3	3	9	1	7
7	7	1	9	3
9	9	7	3	1

G_{12}	1	5	7	11
1	1	5	7	11
5	5	1	11	7
7	7	11	1	5
11	11	7	5	1

There are only two groups of order 4, up to isomorphism, the cyclic group $\mathbb{Z}_4$ and the four-group V. The groups G_5 and G_{10} have generators 2 and 3 respectively, so they are cyclic and isomorphic to $\mathbb{Z}_4$. The elements of G_8 and G_{12}, apart from the identity elements, all have order 2, so these groups are not cyclic, and are isomorphic to the four-group V.

8   The algebra of sets

Exercise 8A (page 94)

1 (a) A (b) B (c) U (d) A
3 (a) $\varnothing$ (b) U (c) U (d) A'

Exercise 8B (page 97)

1 (a) $A \cap B'$ (b) $A \cup B$
2 (a) $\varnothing$ (b) A
   (c) A' (d) $A \cup B$
   (e) $A \cap B$ (f) $A \cap B$
6 (a) $\{1,2,5,6\}$ (b) $\{1,2\}$
   (c) $\{5,6\}$ (d) $\{1,2\}$

7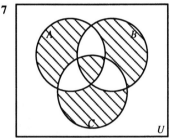

The region representing $A \, \Delta \, (B \, \Delta \, C)$ is symmetrical with regard to the sets A, B and C. This suggests that Δ is associative.

8 (a) $A' \cup B$ (b) U

Review exercise

(page 98)

3 (b) Show that
$$((a,b)*(c,d))*(e,f)=(a,b)*((c,d)*(e,f)).$$
   (c) $(1,0)$
4 (a) $\{y \in \mathbb{R} \mid 0 < y \le 1\}$ or $\,]0,1]$
   (b) Not injective, as $f(1) = f(-1)$; not surjective as no element maps to 2.
   (c) $A = \mathbb{R}^+ \cup \{0\}$ or $A = [\,0,\infty[\,$;
       $B = \{y \in \mathbb{R} \mid 0 < y \le 1\}$ or $B = \,]0,1]$
5 R is an equivalence relation. The equivalence classes are numbers of equal modulus.
6 (a) $\begin{pmatrix} 1 & 2 & 3 & 4 \\ 4 & 3 & 2 & 1 \end{pmatrix}$, $\begin{pmatrix} 1 & 2 & 3 & 4 \\ 3 & 1 & 4 & 2 \end{pmatrix}$

$\begin{pmatrix} 1 & 2 & 3 & 4 \\ 2 & 3 & 1 & 4 \end{pmatrix}$, $\begin{pmatrix} 1 & 2 & 3 & 4 \\ 2 & 3 & 1 & 4 \end{pmatrix}$
   (b) 4, 2

7 (a) $\{1,12\}$ (b) $\{1,3,9\}$
   (c) By Lagrange's theorem, the order of a subgroup divides the order of a group. As 5 does not divide 12, there is no subgroup of order 5.
8 (a) a, 4; b, 1; c, 4; d, 2
   (b) $\{b,d\}$
9 (a) $(b \otimes c)(x) = 1 - \dfrac{1}{1-x} = \dfrac{1-x-1}{1-x} = \dfrac{x}{x-1}$

$d(x) = \dfrac{x-1}{x}$; $e(x) = \dfrac{x}{x-1}$

   (b)

G	i	a	b	c	d	e
i	i	a	b	c	d	e
a	a	i	c	b	e	d
b	b	d	i	e	a	c
c	c	e	a	d	i	b
d	d	b	e	i	c	a
e	e	c	d	a	b	i

   (d) Not commutative as $d \otimes a = b$ and $a \otimes d = e$.
   (e) Not cyclic since it is not commutative.
   (f) $\{i\}$, $\{i,a\}$, $\{i,b\}$, $\{i,e\}$, $\{i,c,d\}$, G

10 (d) $\begin{pmatrix} \pm 1 & b \\ 0 & 1 \end{pmatrix}$

   (e) $\left\{ \begin{pmatrix} 1 & 0 \\ 0 & 1 \end{pmatrix}, \begin{pmatrix} 0 & -1 \\ 1 & 0 \end{pmatrix}, \begin{pmatrix} -1 & 0 \\ 0 & -1 \end{pmatrix}, \begin{pmatrix} 0 & 1 \\ -1 & 0 \end{pmatrix} \right\}$
   This is the subgroup generated by a rotation of $\frac{1}{2}\pi$ anticlockwise about the origin.

12 (b) $\{2\}$, $\{2,5\}$, $\{2,4,0\}$, G
14 In order, 9, 17, 25, 33, 41, 49, 57, 1.
Inverses are in pairs, 9, 57; 17, 49; 25, 41; and 33 is self-inverse.
Generators are 9, 25, 41, 57.

15

	0	1	2	3	4	5	6
0	0	1	2	3	4	5	6
1	1	1	1	1	1	1	1
2	2	1	0	6	5	4	3
3	3	1	6	4	2	0	5
4	4	1	5	2	6	3	0
5	5	1	4	0	3	6	2
6	6	1	3	5	0	2	4

Remove the element 1.

16 $\varnothing$, 1; A, 2; B, 2; $A\Delta B$, 2
17 The equivalence classes are the sets $aH = \{ah \mid h \in H\}$ for each element $a \in G$.

Examination questions

1 (b) $\begin{pmatrix} 1 & 0 \\ 0 & 1 \end{pmatrix}$, $\begin{pmatrix} 1 & 0 \\ 1 & 1 \end{pmatrix}$, $\begin{pmatrix} 0 & 1 \\ 1 & 1 \end{pmatrix}$, $\begin{pmatrix} 1 & 1 \\ 1 & 0 \end{pmatrix}$

  (c) (i) $\begin{pmatrix} 0 & 1 \\ 1 & 0 \end{pmatrix}$ has order 2;

   $\begin{pmatrix} 1 & 1 \\ 1 & 0 \end{pmatrix}$ and $\begin{pmatrix} 0 & 1 \\ 1 & 1 \end{pmatrix}$ have order 3.

  (ii) $\begin{pmatrix} 1 & 0 \\ 0 & 1 \end{pmatrix}$, $\begin{pmatrix} 1 & 1 \\ 1 & 0 \end{pmatrix}$, $\begin{pmatrix} 0 & 1 \\ 1 & 1 \end{pmatrix}$

2 (b) (iii) In $\mathbb{Z}_m$, $p +_m q = p + q \,(\text{mod } m)$

3 (a) Closure is satisfied as the result of multiplying any two members of the set is still a member of the set. d is the identity. The inverses of a,b,c,d,e are respectively a,b,c,d,e. However, $a(be) = ac = e$ and

$(ab)e = ce = a$, so the associative rule is not satisfied. Hence three but not four of the axioms are satisfied.

  (d) (i) $\begin{pmatrix} 2 & 1 \\ 1 & 1 \end{pmatrix}$ (ii) $\begin{pmatrix} 0 & 1 \\ 1 & 0 \end{pmatrix}$

4 (b) $\{2,4,8,10,14\}$ and $\{6,12\}$

5 (a) $\left[e^{-1} - 1, e - 1\right]$

  (b) (i) $f(0) = f(\pi) = 0$

   (ii) Not a surjection; no element maps to 2.

  (c) (i) $\frac{1}{2}\pi$

   (ii) $g^{-1}(x) = \arcsin\left(\ln(1+x)\right)$

   (iii) $\left[-\frac{1}{2}\pi, \frac{1}{2}\pi\right]$

Index

The page numbers refer to the first mention of each term, or the box if there is one.